T0090173

FROM HORSE AND BUGGY TO SPACE

Oscar (Mo) Schaer

ISBN: 978-1-4269-3319-6 (sc)
ISBN: 978-1-4269-3320-2 (e-b)

Library of Congress Control Number:

*Our mission is to efficiently provide the world's finest, most comprehensive
book publishing service, enabling every author to experience success.
To find out how to publish your book, your way, and have it available
worldwide, visit us online at www.trafford.com*

Trafford rev. 06/25/2010

 www.trafford.com

North America & international
toll-free: 1 888 232 4444 (USA & Canada)
phone: 250 383 6864 ♦ fax: 812 355 4082

AUTOBIOGRAPHY
OF OSCAR SCHAER

It is commonly understood that most people remember very little prior to the age of five years. In my case this seems to be normal as I have only a vague image of a very bright light. Mother informed me that at the age of two I was operated on for T A and C and that was very probably the light that I remember. I recall our house, a two story white frame at 774 Kelton Ave, Columbus, Ohio. My first spanking was for trying to stick something into an electrical outlet in the dining room. Mom laid into me and that was the end of experimentation for that day. Next I recall holding my hand in a basin of ice water for a long time. Mother had been ironing and I reached up and laid the palm of my hand on the hot iron. I can still see the blisters on my fingers and palm. At walking age Mother and I visited Fair Wood Ave. Elementary school for a teachers conference for my sister, Christina. The long walk and the wieners and sauerkraut lunch suddenly erupted and ended the session. Not a good day for Mom..

Dad was a Master Wood Pattern Maker and worked out of Columbus most of the time. Norma Bechtold, mothers sister was a Gym Teacher at Mound Jr. High School. At five years I distinctly remember Norma driving us to the doctors for my smallpox vaccination in preparation for entering Kindergarten. After the agony of the needle, we stopped for a Freezy Frozen Chocolate Malted Milk Shake as a consolation prize for my not crying. The vaccination was protected by a clear plastic cover to prevent dirt infection. On the playground some kid grabbed my arm while playing tag and ripped off the cover and the scab that had formed and blood was running down my arm. My sister punched the kid in the nose and the three of us ended up in the principals office. Miss Brown was my teacher and I was always putting my hands in my pockets. One day she said, "Oscar if you don't keep your hands out of your pockets I'm going to pin them to the ceiling !!" The next morning at line up some wise guy said, "Miss Brown I have a pin to pin Oscar's hands to the ceiling." I ran all the way home crying. My Mother, with me in tow, beat feet back to school and settled the matter with Miss Brown out of ear shot of the class.

Our school was at least a half mile from home and one morning we walked by a house that had exploded during the night. It was said that there was a gas leak and the father went down the basement and lit a match. The entire roof was blown off and all windows and doors were broken out. We had a bully that lived a few houses away and when I would go down the alley to the store he would come out and bully me. My dad taught me how to make a good fist and told me to aim for his nose the next time. I did and the blood flew and he ran home screaming. No more bully!!! I had learned a good lesson. Bubby was my nick name and the word was out, "Don't mess with Bubby." All the houses in Columbus had a dirt or gravel alley behind the lots. The gas valve behind our house had a round cast iron lid about 5 inches around with quarter inch holes in the top. A playmate and I were lighting matches and dropping them through the holes. If there had been a leak in the valve we would have been seriously injured had it exploded. Anyway, a trash collector was coming down the alley with his horse and wagon and my playmate said, "Call him a DAGO WOP." I did and the man screamed, "Im'a gona beata your asses" He whipped the horse and we ran. That man chased us with his horse and wagon for a long time. We would jump over a fence and go through the yard to the street and in a few minutes here he would be coming with his whip beating the horse.

A Lutheran Church was in the neighborhood and I was Christened there but have no memory of that event. I do, however remember attending Sunday School. My dad had allowed me to carry his Gold Pocket Watch to church. The front and back of the watch was attached with screw threads. I was fiddling with the watch instead of listening to the lesson and the glass cover came out of the gold frame. I tried to fit it back into the frame and it wouldn't fit. I put it in my mouth and tried to bite it in with my teeth. The crystal broke. My dad was furious and my second licking was the result.

Our house was two stories, kitchen, dinning room and living room downstairs, full basement with a huge coal furnace, bathroom, two bedrooms and a screened summer porch up stairs. Under the back porch was a gated storage area for the wagon, sled, scooter and tricycle. We had a nice back yard to the alley with a garden plot, cherry tree, peach tree, and apple tree. Aunt Norma had given expensive toys to Christina and I that were well made of steel, truck with a screw lifted bed, steam shovel that opened and closed, Lionel electric train and dolls for Chris. We had a very nice comfortable life when the depression developed. Dad was laid off, the real estate companies had foreclosed on many homes and dad made and bought the necessary tools needed to take up the paper hanging trade. He practiced on our house. I remember he was in the upstairs bedroom trying to cover the ceiling with paper. Evidently he had made the paste too thin and the paper was coming down behind him as he was moving forward with the brush. He hollered for Mom to come help him hold up the paper with a broom as he walked across the trestle with the brush. My first lesson in cussing. The air was blue, but he conquered the task and got a few jobs hanging paper in the foreclosed houses. The next door neighbor was a Jewish family and they owned a meat store. My mother cleaned their house on Fridays and the man would give her a sack of meat. I remember dad saying if it hadn't been for those Jews we would have gone hungry many times. Once a week we would walk to the fire house for a bag of flour and beans. The fire truck came down the street at Christmas and handed out toys to the families with children. My dad would not let us have any. Said, we don't want charity. The Hungarians that lived across the street got a whole sack of toys so we got to play with them. My dad said, just like those damned Hunkies to take charity. He was from Switzerland and I guess the Germans and Swiss didn't like the Hungarians. Several blocks away there was a city playground with swings, teeter totters, tall slides, wading pool and ball field. We kids did not notice anything bad about the depression. We just played and did our chores.

My mother related this story to me during a visit when she was dying at age 87. While in the back yard under the cherry tree during the depression she and daddy were discussing their future. She made the statement that she hoped when I grew up, I would have a better job than a Pattern Maker or Paper Hanger to support my family. Dad knocked her down!! I never saw any fighting between them during my lifetime. I came home from the first grade one afternoon and they were both sitting on the couch crying. The finance company had foreclosed and we were going to have to move. Since Aunt Norma was a school teacher and had a job, Dad asked her to borrow the money for a house payment. She tried to tell him that her salary would not allow her to make payments and that since there was no work in sight she could not do it. He got mad at her and told my mother that Aunt Norma should never cross our door step in the future. After the tears and thought, Dad made the statement that a black family had recently moved in up the street and it was just as well that we get out of that neighborhood as within a few years the entire area would be black. A true statement, as the entire east side of Columbus is a getto today. No stores, no shoe shop, no drug stores, no banks, just a getto.

We moved to 266 Miller Ave. into one half of a double two story frame at $14.00 per month rent. This was 1932, mother finally got a job with the city sewing calico shirts to hand out to the poor. Dad was the Chief Cook and Bottle Washer for awhile. Nobody had anything but we were happy. My chores were to stop behind the stores on the way home from school for wooden crates to break up into kindling for the coal stove in the dining room. A ton of coal was $5.00 and I would haul it in two bushel baskets in my wagon from the front curb to the wood shed in the back yard. We kids shoveled snow in the winter and cut grass in the summer. We collected coat hangers and news papers and hauled them in our wagon to the junk yards and dry cleaners for 25 cents for one hundred pounds of papers and 25 cents for fifty coat hangers at the dry cleaners. We ice skated with clamp on skates and roller skated with clamp ons. The rich kids had regular shoe skates!!! Whoopee!! We swam in the creek and played ball in the park and soaped windows and turned over out houses at Halloween!!! We had a pet rabbit, named Dippy, who lived in a cage nailed on the side of the wood shed. Dippy had a bad habit of peeing on people he didn't know. The neighborhood initiation for a new move in was to take him or her over to see our pet rabbit, Dippy. You guessed it, Dippy whirled around and soaked them. LOL!!!!

Christina and I came home for lunch one day and dad had rabbit for lunch. Dippy's pen was empty and dad said he took Dippy to market and traded him for a dressed rabbit. Christina looked in the garbage can and there was the fur from Dippy. Chris cried and could not eat her share. I enjoyed hers and mine!!!!

My Dad was strong and could let me hang onto his little finger and lift me off the ground. I weighed about 90 pounds. The neighbor kid and their dads did not believe my story. I told my dad and he said bring their dads over here to the back fence and I will show them. They came and he lifted me!. Then he told them that if any of them helped the finance companies to move peoples furniture out on the sidewalk he would beat their asses.

Finally dad got on WPA (Works Project Administration) under Roosevelt's presidency. He was paid $16.00 per week as a Foremen with a work crew of six men. They built sidewalks and small fences along the walkways at the Ohio State University, repaired cells and restored facilities at the Columbus Workhouse, etc. His crew was black and he enjoyed those people and said they were more fun to be around than any group of whites. One day at lunch at the workhouse two men ate their lunch inside a cell. When lunch was over he called them for work and said they laughed and stated, "Our liabilities are on the outside but our assets in JAIL". Laughed and leaned on the shovels all afternoon. At Christmas they all chipped in and bought him a can of Prince Albert Pipe Tobacco and a bottle of Whiskey. Dad admitted that his eyes got wet, as none of them had any money to give away. I never again heard any bad remarks about blacks or Jews from my father.

During this depression period my second grade teacher was a round little woman named Mrs. Heintz.. I was a pretty good artist and could draw the NRA eagle (National Recovery Act) and Dick Tracy on the black board. My mother came to visit the second grade and Mrs Heintz ran over and hugged her and told her what an artist I was. Whee!!

This period 1933-1939 was fairly hum- drum. We played in the park, swam in the creek, made boats from orange crates, made roller skate box scooters by nailing the skate wheels to a two by four and nailing an orange crate on the front with two sticks for a handle and pushed ourselves like a scooter. In the winter we ice skated in Franklin Park and slid down the hills on our sleds. We would go down all the alleys past the Oak St. Street Car repair barns and talk to the mechanics who repaired the street cars. Would scour the scrap yard for the steel slugs punched out of the half inch steel plate and use the slugs in our sling shots. There were over a mile of trash cans in the alleys and we would find all kinds of good stuff the people had thrown out. At the end of the car lines the passengers would throw their cigarettes away when the bell rang to get on the car. We would strip the butts and roll our own cigarettes with a Bugler Roller. We had a nice swimming hole between the Broad Street Bridge and the Fair Avenue swinging bridge. Between the Fair Ave. Bridge and the Main Street bridge we had cut a wee narrow path through the weeds and saplings and made a sharp turn about three feet into the brush so that the path was not visible to passers by. Built a nice shack back in the woods and that was our hide out. We could get 2 cents for empty coke bottles. One day Billy Gorslene popped in and said he knew where there were a whole bunch of empty bottles. We filed out like Indians to the rear of the Shell Gasoline Station at Main and Nelson. Everyone was running up to the storage box and grabbing two empty bottles. When I looked in the box, I hesitated, and just then a huge hand lifted me off my feet. We had been caught!! Everybody came back and he called the Bexley Police. (I believe he held the lever down so the call did not go out). He hung up and said we had 15 minutes to round up all the bottles that had been taken. We were pleading that we had some money in our piggy bank at home and would go home and get the money to pay for the bottles. "That's not the point boys, you stole my bottles!!" We finally found all the empties they had thrown in the weeds and he let us go. A LESSON LEARNED, I have never in my entire life ever thought about stealing anything!! Tom Sawyer and Huck Finn had nothing on the Miller and Oak Street Gang. It was Ed and Richard Mavis, Billy Gorslene, Jack Van Keuren, Herman Scott, Paul Gritter (All deceased) and myself. When we got a little older we would write notes to the Kroger Grocer and the Wine Store and would ask for cigarettes and wine for our dad.

The clerks sold the items with no questions and I'm sure they knew the notes had been written by us. We broke out all the lights under the Norfolk and Western railroad viaducts with our sling shots. We would hike the seven miles out to the airport to watch the planes. Our mothers never worried about us as it was seldom heard of anyone bothering children. As long as we were home for supper every thing was fine. The alleys were our playground as there were very few automobiles and that is where we played Ball, Tag, Blind Mans Bluff, Kick the Can, Go Sheepy-Go, Cowboys and Indians, Cops and Robbers using cap guns. On the Fourth of July for two weeks that is all one could hear was fire crackers going off. I won a $10 box of fireworks one year and our whole gang had plenty of bangers. The fireworks stands were at Livingston and Nelson Rd. Across the street were strawberry fields and during the season we would be paid 5 cents a quart to pick the berries.

Most of the back yards had grapes or some type of fruit tree, such as apple, cherry, peach and we would pick a few to chew on. The owners never caught us or thought much of it. We would jump over fences to hide in their yards while playing our games and never got chased away. One garage was completely covered with Ohio License plates as the owner was a guard at the Ohio State Penitentiary. A Junior High School course involved a visit to the Pen so we would know what prison was like and therefore stay away from crime. Some times when an execution was scheduled we would all stand under the street light to see if the lights dimmed at 10 o'clock when they threw the switch. Of course the lights never dimmed!! When the World Champion Boxing Matches were broadcast over the radio we would all stand out in the street listening to some ones radio. (Not every family had a radio) Max Baer, Primo Canero, Max Schmeling, Joe Louis, Billy Conn were some of the top boxers. The rules were no hitting below the belt, break on the clinches, and to kick some one in a fight was never even though of. That was dirty!!!

In the back yard of the Journal Night Green newspaper building, there was a large pile of lead type being saved for remelt. We could fill our pockets and then melt the lead to make our lead soldiers and cowboys. We had molds that could be purchase at the 5 and 10 cent store. We would take Mercury from the chemistry lab at school and cover dimes, quarters and nickels so they would really be shinny. Around the coal stove in the dining room we had a sheet of asbestos 3 feet wide tacked to the wall to prevent fire. On the top of the kitchen stove mothers had a piece of asbestos to set the hot skillets and pans on. All of us have lived into the late 70's or more and have not had any cases of lead, mercury or asbestos poisoning. My mother lived to 87, and Aunt Norma was 93. None of my youthful friends have died of cancer.

In the winter we would listen to Jack Armstrong, the All American Boy, " Eat Wheaties", Orphan Annie, " Drink Ovaltine", Buck Rogers, The Shadow Knows, FBI, Amos and Andy and of course Lum and Abners "Jot 'em Down Store".

During this period of unemployment Dad applied for citizenship. He was told that since mother had married him, she would also need to be naturalized. She married an alien and therefore lost her citizenship even though her parents and she were all born in Columbus, Ohio. I recall there was a ruckus stirred over that ruling but never- theless they both had to take the course and be naturalized. The Certificates are in my son Matt's possession.

I got my skinny tired used bicycle for $12.00 at the age of 10. Work had picked up and my dad was working in Michigan building automobile patterns from wood to make the dies to mold the fenders and body parts. Dad bought his first car, a 1932 Hudson/Terra Plane in about 1936. He taught me how to drive and when he came home every other weekend I would get to drive out in the country.

During the recovery period 1934-42, since Dad was working in Michigan and only came home every other week end, Norma was a regular visitor to the house and many times took us out to eat at a downtown restaurant or on a shopping trip so mother would not have to carry bundles of bags on the long walk from the street car line. Norma purchased an upright piano and paid for Christina's weekly piano lessons. Mothers brother, Uncle Left, name was Theodore Bechtold, and wife Selma with two daughters, Josephine, who was married, and Betty Jean, teenager, lived on the west side of town across the street from the fenced property of the "Nut House". The crazies would look through the tall wrought iron fence and make all kinds of idiotic faces at the people walking along the side walk. We often visited Uncle Left and it was a long street car ride from the east end, with a transfer, to the west side of town. Left was a Roofer and Tinner, and owned a shop on Livingston Avenue. He had a Model T Ford pick up truck that I would sit in, in the garage, and pretend to be driving. He raised rabbits and taught me how to nail them up on the wall, slit their throats, skin them, and dress them for the oven. Selma was a rolly polly "Hill Billy" from Ironton, Ohio that had been raised in the backwoods along "Hog Skin Holler Road". She had numerous superstitions such as," Two people never make a bed" or ""Table scrapes must go to the birds". Her sister would visit once in awhile from Ironton. She smoked a pipe, chewed "Towbaki" played her guitar and spit in an empty coffee can. Wrote a song called "Song Birds of the Woods, they sing the sweetest melody" spit, spit. I used to love to listen to her sing. Josephine's son, my cousin, Ronny, was several years younger than I and he introduced me to all his neighborhood friends. We would play all afternoon and soon would hear, "RONNIE, RONNIE". We would run to the house and be told that he had not been called. The Parrot caged at "Painters" the little confectionary store down the street, had called for Ronnie. Many times Norma would come over later in the day and we would all have a nice meal and songfest while Betty Jean and Christina played the piano. Dad was never the wiser to Norma's visits and he did not say anything about Norma's purchase of the piano. I remember during one visit that Dad was due in from Michigan and Mom was on the edge of her seat for Norma to leave. She said, "No I am going to have it out with that bull head." Mom finally got her to leave out the back door as Dad was coming in the front door. He saw her head pass the dining room window and a few cuss words filled the air for a short time. On his dying bed, he told mom, "That sister of yours can come over." They did make peace before he fell asleep. I had already learned that "Bullheadedness is not for me."

At 14 I was hired to fire the furnaces in a apartment house row across the street from my house. There were six furnaces and I would stoke them in the morning about 6:00AM and get them going and then stoke them after school and again about nine at night. For $15.00 a week. In the summer at age 14 I caddied at the Columbus Country Club. We would hitch hike the seven miles out in the country. Occasionally a queer would try to pick you up but we got to know the bad cars. If we picked dandelions from the fairways we could borrow the members clubs and play a round of golf on Monday mornings. The Pro would go from foursome to foursome giving free instruction. Out of 110 caddies there were three kids who were shooting in the low seventies at the end of the summer. They had the talent. The rest of us were anywhere up to 120 for 18 holes. At 15 I got a part time job at Western Auto Stores for Saturday, working in the garage installing batteries and seat covers. During the summer I worked full time. My next job, at 16, was at the Columbus Army Depot working on a labor gang on Saturdays and then full time the first part of the summer at 50 cents an hour. Christina had gone to work after graduation from East High School and worked for 39 years at the Timken Roller Bearing Plant. She told me they were hiring so I got on at Timkens at 68 cents per hour for the rest of the summer. Dads work at the auto plants had turned to tanks and everyone was back at work. Hitler was on the move and Lend Lease was in progress. We were making and supplying arms to England and Russia and had not yet entered the war. My father finally got a job in Columbus at the Curtiss Wright Corp. and was able to stay at home. He came home sick with a severe back ache. We had moved from the Miller Ave. house to a purchased home at 1484 Bryden Rd., brick with full basement and finished attic, two car garage for a total of $5700. Dad was elated and said this house was much better than the house that had foreclosed. His illness was described as Lumbago and was given a vile tasting liquid that did no good. I drove him to a Chiropractor and he was told he had a severe internal infection and needed a Medical Doctor. Examination revealed infected teeth and since the only medication was Sulfa they could not kill the infection and his blood was so poisoned that the only help was Morphine to ease the pain until he would die. He passed away one month later in December 1943 at the young age of only 57. An interesting side note in the following paragraph.

Mom told me that dad had worked his way over to the United States from Switzerland to attend Ohio State University. He entered through Ellis Island in 1910 at the age of 24. Proceeded to Columbus and worked his way through the Mechanical Engineering Program and graduated from OSU. He then went to work at the Jeffrey Manufacturing Company in Columbus as an apprentice Engineer in the drafting room tracing and correcting drawings.. Worked there six months and was told if he ever wanted to make good in Engineering he should join the Masons. He said, "I left Europe because of Secret Organizations and if I have to join a secret organization you can stuff this job!!" He packed up his equipment and quit the Engineering job and went back to Pattern Making. Talk about BULLHEAD!!! That's not all. Mother said he had a tooth filled and the Dentist charged $5.00 for about 3 minutes work. He told the Dentist, I worked just as long and just as hard as you did for my Degree and that is the last $5.00 you will ever get from me!!!!! He never went back to a Dentist. I once saw him go down the basement, get a pair of pliers, and pull out one of his teeth. His BULLHEADEDNESS did him in!!!

He had taken out a $4000 Life Insurance Policy with Curtiss Wright and got me aside in the living room and told me that he was going to die shortly and that I would have to be the man of the house. He said Mother can pay off the Mortgage from the Insurance Policy but will need help with the other bills. It is up to you and Christina to help out. "I finally screwed somebody with this Insurance Policy because I have only made a few payments." His entire life had been scrimp and save. Shortly after they had married he tried to open a Cabinet Shop in Zanesville, Ohio. It went well for a few months and he finally got stuck with orders that the buyers couldn't pay for. They had to close the shop and he went back to his Pattern Making. I truly believe he died happy.

During this period of my life from 7 to 17 the country had progressed from the horse drawn junk dealer, the Omar Bakery horse drawn cart with the five foot diameter rear wheels, the solid rubber tired fire trucks and trash trucks driven by chain drive, from Model T Fords to nice shinny new cars. Electric and gas refrigerators had replaced the Ice Box. I had graduated from roll your own Bull Durham in the little white bag with the yellow string, to tailor made cigarettes at two packs for a quarter. Walked the mile to school smoking my Yellow Bowl pipe. Hot Stuff!!!! Everybody smoked in those days and every scene in the movies the actors were smoking. My father had traded in the 32 for a 1937 Two Door Ford (New Price $750.00) and from there to a 1940 Nash in which the back seat converted to a bed with screens in the rear windows. He slept in the car while working in Michigan . While we were sitting on the front porch in the evening my mother would send me to the confectionary store for a dimes worth of candy. I would come back with a sack full of Black Babies, so called because they were licorice molded babies, 3 for a penny; Mary Janes, 5 for a penny; a couple of suckers, chewing gum and green leafs. Milk was 11 cents a quart, bread the same for a loaf, and the highest test gasoline (98 octane) was 18 cents a gallon. The 1940 Nash was $850 new and when dad passed mom sold it for $950 in Jan 1944. Had 30,000 miles and was three years old.

The Japanese had bombed Pearl Harbor and all my class mates were going into the service. I stayed with mother for two months and she signed my enlistment papers for the Navy in February 1944 three days before I turned 18. Christina had a steady job at Timkens making 70 cents an hour and mom had the house paid, money from the car and I knew the two of them would have no problems. Every body in the country was for the war and the nation was fully united for the war effort.

My first train ride was to Chicago as a Navy enlistee, it was bitter cold when we arrived at the Great Lakes Naval Base at 2:00AM. The snow crunched under foot and we were fed white navy beans with catsup in the mess hall. Marched over to a building and were given a mattress cover and two blankets and led to a barracks for sleep. One kid said, "I'm getting out of the Navy, I'm going to piss in the bed." He did and the next morning we never saw him again. After the eight weeks of "Boot" camp which covered first aid, drill, rifle, marching, shots, vaccination, gas mask, etc I was told that I scored high on the code test and would be going to Aviation Radioman School at Memphis, TN. We were given ten days leave to go home. Schooling consisted of self defense, disarming, obstacle course, code, semaphore, blinker, aircraft recognition, message construction, first aid, swimming, boxing, wrestling, and numerous other activities of interest. We finally were allowed to go into Memphis on the cattle cars, (Navy Gray trailers with benches on the sides) for the 25 mile ride into town. My friend from Kansas and I bought a bottle of Gin and went to the Peabody Hotel to drink it. The waitress showed us how to make a drink with ice and 7 UP. We drank the bottle, didn't feel any effects and were walking back to the bus station when it hit. We both fell down and were laughing and couldn't get up. Our buddies took us under the arms to the station. We finally got on the bus and on the way back to the base I got sick. An old "SALT" grabbed my white hat and shoved it under my chin. I filled it and he shoved it back on my head. They dropped me off in the shower with the cold water turned on. I finally staggered to the bottom bunk and fell asleep. I have never allowed myself to become helpless since.

From Memphis we were transferred to Naval Air Gunners School east of Purcell Oklahoma for five weeks of 50 calibre machine gun training. The training was completed and there was a back log of students with no place to go. We were given all sorts of odd jobs to occupy our time and finally in December 44 were given 18 days leave to report to Jacksonville, Fl. I worked on the F4U Corsair Flight Line cleaning planes, directing the pilots to their parking spots and just passing time. I was directing one of the newly Commissioned pilots into the parking slot and he raised the Landing Gear, the Corsair hit the ground. Pieces of concrete and metal from the prop were flying every where. One of the new pilots was having trouble starting the engine. They did not have electric starters yet. I had to climb up on the wing and insert a 12 gauge sized cartridge into the starter magazine. When the pilot hit the switch the shell would explode and would turn the engine over. Well, I had climbed up there about five times and finally the First Class Mechanic, who was in charge of we line crewmen, jumped up on the wing and said, "You dumb numskull, you have to turn the gas on!!!!" These pilots had completed their training in the "Yellow Perils", were commissioned Ensigns, but it was their first time in a powerful war plane. They were all very nervous on their first flight.. When the pilot got back he sought out the First Class and ordered him up to the Commanding Officer's office. The Skipper excused the First Class and we could hear the Captain chewing out the Ensign. That was the old Navy. Today Politically Correctness has taken over.

My first flight for earning flight pay was in the rear of the PBY Catalina Flying Boat. Twenty one dollars a month plus flight pay, WOW!! I sent Mom half of my pay each month. In January 45 I was finally assigned to a four engine bomber squadron as Tail Gunner and Third Radioman. We were in training at a small field, named Crows Landing just north of Modesto, CA and were slated to go to China. The entire squadron was given every shot and vaccination the Navy had and we were all sick for two days with arms and butts sore from the shots. Guess What!!! Sorry Men, orders are cancelled. Transferred to Camp Kearney, CA which is now Miramar and we lined up every morning for muster behind the plane captain who was a First Class Mechanic. There were nine men in each crew and over 200 crews were backed up at Miramar. The three Aviation rates for flight crews were Mechanics, Radiomen and Ordnance men. Every third day we got liberty to go off base while the other two rates did the work. The war soon ended and we were sent to Kaneohe Bay Naval Air Station in Hawaii. Discharged in February 46.

One interesting little sea story happened at Naval Air Station Jacksonville in the time frame that FDR died at Hot Springs, GA.. We were standing in the pay line and a newly Commissioned Ensign was checking every ones pay chit. A First Class Petty Officer was ahead of me and the Ensign found a mistake on the old "SALTS" pay chit. He raised his voice and hollered, "How long have you been in the Navy, **SAILOR**?" answer, "**ELEVEN YEARS**, How many **DAYS** have you been in, **SIR**." For your information, during the war, They had a 90 day training curriculum for men with some college background. They were then Commissioned as Ensigns. We referred to them as "90 Day Wonders"

I enjoyed ever minute of my Navy Service, met many good, honest people and we were all 100% American. I would not trade that experience. I was disappointed that I did not get involved in the fighting. When the war ended and we were transferred to Kaneohe Bay I thought, "Now I will get to see the bombed out hangers and ships at Pearl Harbor". A great disappointment, upon arrival at Pearl, Every thing was ship shape and there was no evidence that any bombs had ever fallen there. All the Palm Trees were blowing in the wind, the buildings were standing and the might of America had renovated the destruction to better than it's Pre-War condition. Whoops, another Sea Story!!

The Natives near Pearl Harbor Naval Base were upset that the sailors were dating their girls and invading their Island. They would step out of a Pool Hall and throw a ball at the sailors passing by, muggings were in vogue. The Policemen would fine the sailors for Jay Walking and arrest them for no particular reason. In late 1945 there occurred a real honest to goodness riot. All the sailors had had enough and went into town and cleaned house. Again the old Navy. Today (2010) the Leadership would punish the sailors and apologize to the muggers. My souvenirs of service were two tattoos. A hula dancer on my calf and a sailing ship on my arm.

Unemployment was rampant after the war and there were few jobs to be had. Veterans were entitled to 52 weeks of unemployment compensation at $20 per week and it was called the 52/20 Club. All my buddies from school and neighborhood were on the dole. We played golf 2 or 3 times a week at 75 cents for 18 holes, drank beer in the evenings at 10 cents a glass and tried to find any type work, which was nil.

I finally got a job at Pennsylvania Rubber Company and worked there during the summer of 46, at which time I returned to Ohio State University in Mechanical Engineering on the GI Bill. (I had completed two quarters after High School.) There was an old man working in the engine repair shop named Pud, (like pudding). I smashed my thumb on a box and he came over and grabbed my hand.. He wrapped his hand around my thumb and said, "Now it's going to get real warm, it did, now it's going to cool off, it did. Now it doesn't hurt. It didn't. I asked if that was hypnosis, he said I don't know what it is but I talk to those things that tell you to look out and there was a car that would have hit you. When you go home tonight ask your mother where she has head aches. I'll tell you she has them right in the top of her head, not on the side, not in front, but on the top of her head. WOW!! Mom confirmed that he was correct. That is the one and only incident I have had with a seer!!!!

ROWBOAT TRIP

While growing up and swimming in the creek we used to build these little boats from boxes taken from the trash behind the stores. Always said we would like to just go down the river. I ran into two buddies that I had known in grade school at Ohio State. We renewed old acquaintances and decided that during the summer lull we would buy a boat and go down the river to New Orleans. We did just that. Paid $297 for an Aluminum row boat and in the summer of 1947 rowed away from the foot of the dam on the Scioto River at Broad Street in Columbus. The Columbus Dispatch said to send them a collect wire from every major city on the entire trip and they would publish the story. Myself, Mack Martin and Don Strader departed on flood water in June of 47. We intended to build a fire each night and cook some soup and baked beans and catch fish and live off the river. We had $30 dollars each, one box of Heintz Baked Beans, one box of Campbells Soup and off we went. The river was high and the current was fast, some where around Chillicothe we sailed right over a dam with just a slight dip in the water. Spent the night in a field and reached the Ohio River at Portsmouth on the second day. Our building a fire and cooking our food went by the wayside as the river banks were solid mud and all firewood was wet from the flood water. We hid the boat and bought some hot dogs and food.

The Ohio River was rolling along at a good pace and we sailed free and easy past Cincinnati. The river is tricky and you will be moving along nicely and suddenly the current has disappeared and you are dead in the water. We took turns rowing and would switch seats every half hour or so. Finally made a fire and evidently there was some flint stone in the rocks. Chips started flying out of the fire and cut my arm. It was a sliver of flint from the hot rock that had exploded off like a projectile. By the time we scrubbed the skillet and cleaned everything up we decided that we would just stop and buy our food. An interesting note was that as the river receded every twig on every small branch on every limb had a condom hanging off. Thousands of condoms for miles and miles along the river banks. At Evansville, Indiana we slept in a farmers barn and he told us that he always set out fishing lines along his property and had caught a 110 pound Catfish one time that measured 12 inches across the eyes. He was extremely nice and the only requirement was no smoking in the barn. We hailed a barge in the middle of the river and they pulled us up on the deck and we rode with them for about twenty miles. That was the only time we did not row ourselves. The Ohio river is not too deep at points and there are dams that can be lowered during flood stage and then raised during low water so as to provide a nine foot depth for river barges. The dams are made up of "Wickets" that can be raised and lowered for this purpose. Only one dam was raised on the Ohio river and we had to go through the locks. The operator allowed us to spend the night on the concrete floor of the dam house and explained that since the river is a natural waterway for transportation they had to lock a boat through for no charge. The law allows them to make you wait up to one hour for other traffic to save money, but if no other traffic arrives they must let you through the locks. He also told us that the fish that had jumped in the boat in the middle of the night and scared us to death was a Gar Fish. We three had never seen or heard of that type fish. It flipped off one of our oars in the middle of the night and was flopping around in the boat. We finally found a flash light and saw this long snout and learned about GAR Fish. The operator at the Dam House told us that we were not doing anything unusual. As soon as school is out for the summer there are all types of boats, rafts, canoes, etc. going down the river. Later in our voyage, on the Mississippi, we were told that a young man had floated from St Louis past his farm in a regular wash tub surrounded with a truck sized inner tube. At Cairo, Illinois, the Ohio joins the Mighty Muddy Mississippi and the current was strong. We were advised to stay on the Missouri side of the river as there was a very strong whirlpool on the Kentucky side that could suck our little rowboat down into the vortex. The current swings back and forth and the pilots know all the little quirks to stay in the current going down river and avoiding the current coming up river. At Caruthersville, MO we were broke. We hid the boat in the brush and got a job Chopping Cotton for the afternoon. We went to work with a gang of negro Cotton Choppers who were singing and chanting as they chopped along the row. The idea was to take a hoe and chop off the weeds growing among the cotton plants so they would not steal the moisture or crowd out the cotton. I had the drizzlies and started chopping faster as I felt I had to go. I left Mack, Don and the singers in the dust and finished my row. The foreman, a young black fellow came over as I was hiding behind the truck in agony, and said, "Boss man Sealy don't want no layin' down on the job." I told him I was sick and he went away. We all got paid the same amount $1.80 and spent it that evening at a restaurant. Slept on the levee that night and left in the boat in the morning. I was still running and we were close to shore and I was rowing. I had to go so I squatted over the side which pined down the oar, and let loose. Mosquitos the size of a fly were all over us. Don and Mack were hollering," Get your ass off the oars and lets get out of here". It was hilarious!!!!. We finally got out away from the shore and left the itchers behind!

We pulled into Memphis, slept on the wooden planking by the boat, got eaten up with mosquitos and wired home for $30 bucks each. Tried to find work at construction sites, boat docks or —any where? When you are dirty and down and out no one wants anything to do with you. We got our money and headed down stream. That night along the Arkansas border we were hugging the shoreline on the west side of the river and approaching a bend to the right. The light from a river boat search light suddenly hit the trees along the shore line ahead of us. We decided to pull into a recess in the embankment just for safety. It was fortunate that we did, as within just a few minutes the front end of a three string river barge coming upstream moved past our spot. Had we stayed the course we would have been run over by the barge and surely would have drowned. The tug pilot was avoiding the down stream current which had crossed over to the other side on the curve. We slept atop the Levee that night. At Greenville, Mississippi we wanted to go into town. We pulled over to the bank and started tromping through the woods to the east. As we stepped over a fallen tree we saw a black snake about 3 inches in diameter lying on the ground. The only snake seen on the entire trip. Couldn't find the town. We back tracked to the boat and a man came up with a wooden boat in which he had installed a six cylinder Chevy engine. H told us that he would tow us into the town. We gave him a line and off we went straight toward the trees, into which he had cut out a path about 5 feet wide, at ten or fifteen miles per hour. The path turned and twisted and at times we thought the front of our boat would swing out and hit a tree and turn us all over. However we came out into a nice wide river and discovered that Greenville is actually hidden from the main stream of the river by an island that we had just flown over. We had a couple of hot dogs and went on our way. The man earned his living by hauling in logs floating down the river. He would retrieve the logs and sell them to the saw mill. When not catching logs he would tend to his fishing lines and said that at times would catch as many as fifty pounds of fish a night.

We had been told that the Corps. Of Engineers, U,S. Army had charts of the entire river that could be purchased. We had mailed an order for the charts and picked them up while at Memphis. They are very detailed, had we researched prior to our departure we could have had the charts for the entire trip. The Mississippi has no dams or locks that we had to go through and is over 200 feet deep in spots. The spring floods had turned the river into brown water and the people living along the banks on house boats would fill a gallon glass jar and let it sit until the mud settled and then we assumed would drink it or boil it further. We saw some jars that had 2 inches of mud in the bottom. If we rowed, way, on the boat and shipped the oars you could hear the dirt rasp along the bottom of the aluminum.

We arrived at the foot of Canal Street in New Orleans after 33 days and 1725 miles of travel from Columbus. Soon learned that if we rowed the boat through the Industrial Canal to Lake Pontchartrain we would have a good chance to sell the boat. We left it moored at the foot of Canal St. and spent the night at the Salvation Army where we showered, washed our clothes and got a good nights sleep in a bed. No one wants to have anything to do with a dirty, unshaven, bum. We found that out in a hurry. We tried to find work at the shipping docks? "Sorry this is a Union Job." Pedaling a White Yummy Ice Cream Cart ? "Do you have a $50 deposit?" Rowed through the canal to the lake and had pulled the boat onto the bank and were using the sand to scrape off the caked on brown dirt from the river trip. A man came over in a dinghy and told us that he had heard about our trip and that we could sleep on his sail boat until we sold the boat. His Schooner had 3 bunks and we still had our uneaten soup and beans. In hog heaven!!!

Our benefactor was about 40 years old and his left arm was encased in a leather cuff from the elbow to the wrist and buckled on with three straps. He explained that he had been riding his motorcycle and approaching a red light he caught the left crash bar on the bumper of a car. The bike fell over and his left arm was shattered between elbow and wrist. The bone was splintered and could not be knitted back together. He was able to raise his sails by a straight pull of up to 75 pounds but could not do anything that would bend his arm. His wife was a school teacher and had "High Falutin' friends" and he had his sail boat and his sailing buddies. He had bummed and sailed all over the seas and knew what it was to be down and out. We stayed on his boat and searched high and low for some type of employment.. On a Wednesday night he took us to the French Quarter to his home. We had steak, baked potato, salad and wine. About 8 o'clock the phone rang and a couple, with whom he had sailed with, were at the Railroad Station. They had sold their boat in Key West and were laying over the night awaiting a further train ride to their home in San Diego. We drove down, brought them to the house, pulled out their guitar, and spent the rest of the night singing and telling stories. It was just a wonderful get together with a bunch of bums!!!!! On a Friday afternoon we convinced an employer, by showing him newspaper clippings of our trip, that we three Ohio State University students would be on his loading dock at eight o'clock Monday morning to load 55 gallon drums of Sorghum Molasses onto trucks for shipment, and would stay on the job until September when school started. His name was Mr. Boudrie. He was hesitant!!! We were insistent!!! We were hired!!!! We sold the boat for $180 on Sunday afternoon, sincerely thanked our benefactor, and hitch hiked westward at 8 the next morning. Our rational for pulling a Boudrie was that it was late on Friday afternoon and he would not have been able to hire any one at that time anyway. To this date, Mack and I laugh about, " Pullin' a Boudrie!!!!!" Don has passed away.

HITCH HIKING JUNKET

In 1947 the roadways were two lanes and only on occasion would you find a three lane. The Pennsylvania Turnpike was the only Toll Road I had heard of. Two lane roads were all there were as we set our sights on Colorado. Don's younger brother was stationed at Lowry Air Force Base near Denver and that was to be our first destination. We soon realized that three bums together would never get a ride. The decision was made to split up, two would stay together and the other would go alone. We would meet at the City Limits sign for the next leg, taking turns to be the lone ranger. This worked out well and we visited all the major cities from New Orleans, through Shreveport, into the vast state of Texas. Continuing north west from Dallas and Ft. Worth into the "Pan Handle" and "Wheat Country" of Dalhart and Dumas. We had all gotten together and were on the side of the road when a farmer asked if we wanted work. He told us that the wheat harvest had filled all the storage silos and they had to pile the wheat up in the field on the grass. The piles were diminished and there remained hundreds of bushels of wheat in the grass. Wheat was selling for $3.00 per bushel and he was willing to pay us $1.00 per bushel to rake and brush the wheat out of the grass and take it to the mills. We piled in his pick up and his wife prepared a nice evening meal for the three of us and we slept in the field by their house. We worked three days and recovered

90 bushels for a net of $30.00 each. Don wanted to see his brother so he left alone the next morning and we had agreed to meet him at the southern city limits sign at Pueblo, Colorado on a particular day.

Mack and I followed a north west heading, we spent the night in a steel jail cell at Raton, New Mexico. It was reputed to have been occupied by Billy the Kid. However research from the Internet does not indicate that Billy the Kid was ever jailed in Raton. His actions were further south in the North eastern part of the state. We proceeded north through Trinidad and to our rendezvous point south of Pueblo. We met at the prescribed time and the three of us, using our two and one cycle were standing near the railroad tracks on the east side of Holbrook, AZ awaiting a ride. A man asked if we wanted to help unload water melons from a freight car sitting on the siding. We made a few dollars for several hours work and then split to rendezvous later at my Aunts in Tucson. Mack and I got a lift from a farm hand who was returning from working the wheat harvest that he had followed up to the Canadian border. We headed south down into the Salt River Canyon which is a beautiful drive descending gradually through Snowflake and Show Low to the low point, at which there is a filling station and restaurant. The auto was getting hot and the driver mentioned that since it was down hill we could make it to the service station. He was drinking beer all the while but was in complete control. He mentioned, however that all he would need was a wrench but that he knew "these people" and they would probably not lend him one, but would sell him one. That is the way it worked out. The service station man said the reason was that too many people had asked to borrow and then drove off with his tools.

So there are always two sides to a problem. (Lesson). We took a refreshment and continued up out of the canyon into the town of Globe, Arizona, arriving at dusk. We found a small patch of grass and gravel in front of a lonely church and had retired for the night. At some late hour we were awakened by a Policeman who informed us that we were in a dangerous spot and would likely wake up in the morning with a lump on our heads and nothing but a pair of shorts. He took us to the police station and we again spent the night safely tucked away in the Globe Jail. There are more GOOD people than bad!!!!! It was my turn to travel alone and I caught a ride into Tucson. The driver was upset that the auto behind us was following too closely and would hit him if he had to stop," like right now, Bang." The damage was slight, however the police took all our names and I went on to Aunt Anna's address. Met with Mack and Don . Anna threw all our dirty duds into the laundry and ordered us to bathe. We were so dirty that you could scrape your finger nail down each others back and leave a white streak in the grime. Anna fed us well, cleaned our clothing, and after two days we were on the road again. Our next stop was Boulder Dam to the north. (Name has been changed to Hoover Dam) We had trouble getting a ride so Mack and I decided to hop a freight train, Don wanted no part of that. We road the rails and hitch hiked past Casa Grande and Phoenix into Blythe, California. Spent the night behind a billboard and proceeded to Needles, CA. Stood on the road side all morning without a ride. Mack and I hopped a freight going west to Barstow and then rode another freight back to Boulder. At Barstow we ran into a young hiker who said that when he ran out of money he would order a plate of fried potatoes, and when the waitress went to the kitchen he would run out the door and hide. None of that for we three. We also met a permanent BUM. This gent was very clean and neatly dressed with a sports car cap, cleanly pressed khaki shirt, creased trousers and clean shaven. He explained he just loved to bum around and would get two cardboard boxes. Lay out his clothes between them and sleep on top. His shirt and pants looked as though they had just come from the dry cleaners. He went north in the summer and Florida in the winter. The railroad detective told us where to catch the next freight to Boulder. He told us that he ate every morning in the café we had just come from, and that he ordered the same meal every morning. " Two eggs, sunny side up, two strips of bacon and two slices of toast". Said he went in there yesterday and the waitress said, "I just scratched what you wanted!!". He replied, "Fine, wash your hands and bring me two eggs, bacon and toast!! "Lots of Laughs".We hopped the freight, spent the night in the jail at Boulder and the three of us took the tour of Boulder Dam the next day. Las Vegas was the booming Gambling Town and we stuck a few nickels into the slots with no success. We headed for the coast at Los Angeles and followed the coastline north to San Luis Obispo and on to San Francisco. Don had the address of an old Navy buddy and we spent the night and refreshed and visited the city the next day. We had enough bumming and decided to head for Columbus. At Sacramento we slept behind a bill board. In the morning, Don said he was heading east and left us. We found out later his first ride was all the way Chicago. He beat us home by three days.

Mack and I jumped on a freight at Elko, Nevada. The doors were closed so we climbed up on the roof. Sitting there dumb, fat and happy and noticed a tunnel ahead that appeared to be just a few inches higher than the roof of the freight. We clamored down the ladder between the cars and hung on. Smoke got so thick we were choking and gasping for air. Fortunately we broke out of the tunnel. A few miles further, another tunnel. This time we hooked our arms through the rungs of the ladder so that if we passed out we would not fall onto the rails and be run over. Three such tunnels on the way to Ogden, Utah. We jumped into one open box car and there were nine other hobos already on board. Several looked as if they would steal the pennies from a dead man's eyelids. We took turns sleeping on that ride. Made our way across Wyoming, Nebraska, Iowa and Illinois to Chicago. At just 45 miles from home, coming into Springfield, Ohio we were riding in the front seat with the driver. We both saw the rails of a concrete bridge and a curve to the left beyond the bridge. A large semi truck was coming around the bend. The driver was smoking his pipe and we were barreling ahead at 70 miles per hour. We finally alerted the driver and he slammed on the brakes, knocking his pipe out of his mouth and hot ashes into our laps as we were skidding into the two lane bridge with the truck radiator looming into our faces. The cab flipped out of our way and the rear trailer wheels just missed the car. The car stopped just before the right fender hit the concrete railing on our side. The driver pulled through the bridge and off the road and stopped. He said I must have been asleep, thank god you boys were with me!!. We sat there for at least five minutes before he drove us on into Springfield.

I had been home long enough to clean up get a good nights sleep in a bed and my other friends asked if I wanted to go to the Cleveland Air Races . Kissed mom on the cheek and went out the door as she was telling me that I was "Just a neer-do-well bum!! You won't amount to a tinkers damn!" "You've been gone all summer, Get a Job!!". Fall Quarter started on the 10th of September and we were back to normal!!

BACK TO SCHOOL

After Graduating from East High School in June of 1943 I wanted to join the Navy. All my class mates were gung-ho to kill the Japs. My father was determined that I was going to Ohio State and marched me down to the bank, forced me to withdraw from my savings account, took me to the Registrar at the University and enrolled me in the Mechanical Engineering Curriculum. On the main floor in the Engineering Building a twenty foot long black board was full of letters indicating that the representative of various companies would be on campus to interview graduates for future employment. I had completed the first quarter when Dad passed away. I gave Mother two months to get over the death and dropped out of school to enter the Navy. Upon discharge from the Navy I re-entered Ohio State on the GI Bill. Mack, Don and I were in the same classes and thus the boat trip. The Engineering Degree had increased from four to five years as a result of the war. My major interest was in the Science courses, I was a whiz at Math and am a member of PI MU EPSILON a National Mathematics Honorary Society. Economics, Geography, Political Science, etc did not draw my attention and I would find myself doodling in the note book during those type classes.

Sometime during 1948 we three, Don, Mack and I purchased motorcycles and expanded our horizons beyond the local neighborhood. We all worked during the summer.

Prior to the fall Quarter a close friend, Don Robbins, and I took a cross country tour across the northern part of Ohio, Niagra Falls, up state New York and back through Washington D.C. I distinctly remember climbing to the top of the Washington Monument. Our vehicle was a 1938 four door Dodge. The ME curriculum required a ten week period of employment in an Engineering Industry. In the summer of 1949 I went to work at United States Steel in Munhall, Pennsylvannia. My assignment was to collect some 62 samples of all the lubricants used throughout the complex. The purpose was to familiarize myself with all aspects of making steel products from the open hearth furnaces to the final products such as steel plate, rail road rails, steel piling, etc. I had to climb up into the over head cranes, on and about the various rolling mills, the open hearth furnaces, blast furnaces and every nook and cranny that I could find the samples. Pay was $1.35 per hour and the experience was vast. I saw the 300 inch metal lathe used to manufacture Battle Ship 16 inch Gun Barrels, huge 5 foot by 5 foot and twenty foot long columns of steel, for Cyclotron construction, being finished off on Milling Machines. A ten thousand word essay was a course requirement. My summer was spent on that project with an occasional hitch hike back and forth to home.

Mack and I had ten days before the Fall Quarter. We strapped a sleeping bag to our cycles and headed for Quebec. It was beginning to cool for fall and our legs were getting cold. A fellow cyclist we met suggested that we wrap our legs with newspaper, pull our jeans over the top, and the problem was solved. We came south into Maine and down the coast to New York, Philadelphia, Baltimore, Washington and arrived home in time for school. After

World War II employment began to gradually simmer down. In January 1950, that same black board in the Engineering Building had only one letter. It was from the Saudi American Oil Company with height and weight requirements and a three year contract. Mack, Don and I had all been in the Navy and we went to the movie, "Task Force". An action packed movie about Naval Carrier action. Don said, "The hell with this Engineering, I'm going to be a Naval Aviator". We drove to the Office of Naval Officer Procurement in Cincinnati, Ohio and were told that after passing the physical and three simple tests in Chicago we could be in Pensacola by February. We completed the entry requirements, dropped out of school, and were in Naval Aviation Cadet Training at Pensacola by the end of February 1950.

FLIGHT TRAINING

We were entered in Class 5-50 at the Naval Air Station, Pensacola, FL. In June of 1950 we were all called into the auditorium and told that due to budget cuts and reductions in size of the military that one third of us would be permitted to finish the 18 month program and would be allowed to stay on active duty. One third would be permitted to finish training, receive our Commission and be released to the inactive reserves. It was hoped that those persons would join a week-end warrior reserve outfit and keep up with their flying. The remaining third could come up to the stage, register their names and orders to their homes would be forthcoming within a few days. Mack elected to go home. Don and I stayed the course. Just a few weeks later the Korean War began and it was, "Balls to the wall." After eight weeks of Pre-Fight, covering Navy Organization, all forms of Navigation including Celestial, Meterology, Ordnance, Aerodynamics, Marching, Formations, Sports, Swimming, and the upside down underwater cockpit escape, (Dilbert Dunker) and the Blue Link Trainers we were ready to get in the cockpit. Our plane was the SNJ, front and rear cockpit (Air Force AT6). Basic training consisted of Stages A through G, which covered Basic Instruction, Solo Flights, Acrobatics, Cross Country, Formation, Tactics, Gunnery, Instruments, and finished with Field Carrier Landing Practice and six Carrier Landings. Don and I sailed through nicely. We then transferred to Corpus Christi, TX and entered Advanced Training in the F6F Hellcat, a World War II Fighter. Cabaniss Field was the location for the F6F Hellcat, AD Sky Raider and F8F Bearcat. Our class had been sorted into Carrier- type, Multi-engine, and Sea Planes. The syllabus was extensive and covered all phases of fighter type aircraft, including live firing of ammunition, bombs, rockets, Final graduation and Commissioning as Ensign with Navy Wings of Gold was our reward after 12 Carrier Landings in the Operational Type Planes. That event occurred on 29 August, 1951 aboard the USS Monterey a Light Carrier. Total First Pilot Time 223 hours.

So that newly commissioned Naval Aviators enter the Atlantic or Pacific Fleet completely qualified regardless of weather the program then called for five weeks of All Weather Flight Training at the Naval Air Station Corpus Christi. Instrument training was conducted in the SNB Twin Engine Beach Craft. A regular evening and week end gathering spot was ZACKIES DRIVE IN on Water Street.. (Name is now U and I). It was THE PLACE to meet the girls of Corpus. The Girls would drive through slowly and then come back and park. Most of the Ensigns were without their own cars and would strike up conversation with the ladies. We were called "Fender Lizards" as we jumped in and out of different cars to find a date. I spotted a young lady that ignited a spark that never faded through her passing after 52 years in 2003. Miss Billie Jeanne George!!! She was IT for me and I proposed marriage prior to leaving Corpus armed with a Standard Instrument Rating to join the Atlantic Fleet. We made plans to join up and marry at a future date. On our way to Columbus, on leave to join the Atlantic

Fleet, Don decided that if I was going to marry Billie, he was going to marry Wilma, a lady he had dated in our home town. My mother was of the "Old School" and a divorced woman with a five year old son was a hard nut to swallow. She was not very receptive to my marriage. However I was 25 years old and had made my choice. We reported into the Atlantic fleet and had two choices for a squadron, Atlantic City flying the World War II F4U Corsair, or Quonset Point, Rhode Island flying the AF2S and AF2W. We had never heard of that type airplane but upon hearing it was a new plane developed during the later stages of the war we elected to go to the newer type planes. First, however we attended school in Norfolk, Va learning about the electronic equipment in the plane, the ordnance carried, the tactics involved, and capabilities of the submarine. The AF's were used for Anti-Submarine Warfare (ASW) and operated as a team with the W Model carrying a very powerful radar that could pick up a submarine periscope from 40 miles distance in a white cap sea state. The S Model had a small attack radar to home in on the selected target, a periscope in the belly of the plane, with a 70,000,000 candle power search lite to illuminate the target for dropping depth charges or torpedoes on the enemy. Both models were single piloted with two aircrewmen in the fuselage. The original war time design was to have been an attack aircraft with the propeller driven engine in the nose and a jet engine in the fuselage. The war ended and the aircraft was redesigned for ASW.

Don had wed Wilma, Billie arrived in Norfolk and we were married by a Justice of the Peace on December 22, 1951. The ceremony was performed in the JP's court room. He quietly and softly asked, "Are you, Oscar Schaer, the person who is named on this Wedding License?" I replied, "Yes." and "Are you, Billie Jeanne George, the person who is named on this Wedding License? She replied, "Yes." He then softly said, "Very well then, everything is in order and we will proceed with the ceremony." He was standing behind the Lectern containing a very large Bible. His eyes rolled up into his head, he raised his head to the ceiling and bellowed out, "By the Powers Vested in me by the Commonwealth, of the State of Virginia" I was shocked and Billie Jumped!! We held on to each other and suppressed our laughter throughout the ceremony!!!

ASW Schooling was completed and we both found acceptable housing in Rhode Island. Don and I checked into Air Anti-Submarine Squadron TWENTY FOUR at Naval Air Station Quonset Point, Rhode Island. Our Commanding Officer's greeting was, "In this Squadron we fly your asses off. The flight schedule is mandatory. Check with your Chief and your men, assist where needed, and get the hell out of here and go home to your wife. We go to sea a lot. Any questions? You are excused!!" We were given a Handbook for the plane, scheduled for familiarization flights of the area, touch and go landings, and commenced Field Carrier Landing Practice for an upcoming cruise. The cockpit was 13 feet above the deck. It was the largest single engine stick plane in the Navy and had wrested that claim from the WWII TBM Torpedo Plane. We would be flying off the smallest carriers, CVE (Carrier Escort) and CVL (Carrier Light) flight Decks. These carriers had been built during the war and were used to escort convoys across the Atlantic to protect against the German Uboat.

It was fun flying as we never got over 1000 feet and our training involved constant breaking off of the S from the

W Model and then, after the simulated attack, a running rendezvous to join up and search for another target. We became adept at formation flying and buzzing the beaches from Atlantic City to Cape Cod. The people would wave and occasionally we would sneak under the Jamestown Bridge at night. Air Group 7, was flying Jet Aircraft and one of their pilots buzzed his girl friend's house at Groton, Connecticut one evening. The windows rattled and her father drove to Quonset the next morning hunting for the culprit. About the same time frame a Jet Jock in Miami buzzed along the main drag about the third floor window level. A Chief of Naval Operations edict was issued and any pilot caught buzzing would face a Pilot's Disposition Board and be stripped of his wings. The fun was over, Safety of Flight was demanded from then on!!!

Our first Cruise was aboard the USS WRIGHT, CVL 49 in April of 1952. Don and I had successfully completed our daylight schedule and the night flights were having trouble landing due to rain and lightning. One LT asked, "Where's the Duty Cat???" He instructed Ensign Irlandi, an artist of sorts, how to draw the cat on the black light board. It is a Black Cat facing away from you and looking back with it's tail raised. A cross on it's butt with a bolt of lightning striking the cat. Irlandi drew the cat and suddenly the pilots started getting their cuts. From then on the Duty Cat was the first thing drawn on the board as long as I was in VS24. The Black Cat shoulder patch was only issued to pilots who were day and night carrier qualified. During the Korean War many reserve pilots were called into active duty. We had received four of these Lieutenants and one Lieutenant Commander who was the new Executive Officer. His past flight experience had been with Multi-Engine Transport type aircraft. Carrier aviation was not to his liking. He finally was night qualified at Sun Set. Ensign Irlandi and another Junior Officer flew down to Norfolk and had a Duty Cat Patch with Sun Glasses on the Cat and a large Red Sun Setting in the background. At morning quarters on the Hanger Deck he was presented with this shoulder patch. He became very irate and all the junior officers were targeted to try and find out WHO had originated that disgusting display toward a Senior Officer. He threatened to Court Martial those involved. Only the guiding hand of the Commanding Officer put a stop to his insanity. Another DingBat!!!

Our first cruise in January 1953 was aboard the USS GILBERT ISLAND (CVE 107) to Guantanamo, Cuba for ASW Training and night carrier qualifications. Sixty day landings were required before starting night carrier landing. Don and I qualified on that cruise and to this day I swear I never could see the deck, just the paddles giving me the cut and the dark outline of the island structure to my right. I had faith in the Duty Cat!!! I burned oodles of Adrenaline during that night. On 23 April 1953 operating off the USS WRIGHT involved in a few refresher landings I felt a surge type movement in the aircraft while proceeding up wind after a landing. I thought something isn't right and snugged up my shoulder straps. Every thing sounded right and the gages indicated normal readings. At the 180 degree position coming down wind to the carrier the procedure was landing check off list, gear down, flaps down, hook down, canopy open, mixture rich, and props in low pitch. At that instant the entire airplane started violently shaking and I experienced a loss of power. I increased throttle with no result, I was at 125 feet, on speed and losing power, I radioed MAY

DAY MAY DAY, SEVEN DECENDENT, DITCHING, started the gear up and landed into seven foot swells. It was exactly as we had been taught in Flight Training. A violent jolt as the plane hit the water, hands, legs and head flying forward, followed by a short skip and the second final jolt with my head going forward another six inches, I know. I followed the taught procedure, got out on the wing, thought I better get the life raft, grabbed the two parachute leg straps to the raft turned and went out to the wing tip, jumped in, turned and paddled back away from the plane. At that time the Helicopter Plane Guard was over head and lowered the horse collar. I remember my fingers were very cold trying to pull the toggles on the life jacket. I reached up into the horse collar, was pulled up into the helo, and was deposited on the flight deck in what I was told a total of 37 seconds. The water was 48 degrees and fortunately we had been issued the MK4 Exposure Suits. The flight surgeon was on deck and they ordered me to lay down in the wire stretcher. I insisted I was okay and the flight surgeon and a corpsman put me in the basket. They banged my elbow going through a hatch on the way to sick bay and I got out of the stretcher and walked the rest of the way. That was the only injury. I was flying again that afternoon. The skipper told me to claim a flight jacket. I said, " I wasn't wearing one." He said, "I saw you wearing it Ensign Schaer!!. "Yes Sir!!"

Prior to the flight during the briefing the squadron flight surgeon sitting next to me heard me say, "Man this suit makes you feel like a Martian. I wonder if it works!!" He swears I ditched the plane just to test the suit. I said, "Doc do you think I would risk my life and ditch a $750,000 plane to test this suit. I would just jump off the pier back at Quonset." I reasoned the violent vibration was due to a chunk of a propeller blade that may have broken off, the mechanics suggested a cracked or broken magneto drive shaft. We will never know as the plane sank in over 10,000 feet of water in the North Atlantic Ocean. Our squadron log book entries always opened with the words, " Air Anti-Submarine Squadron TWENTY FOUR temporarily based ashore at Naval Air Sation Quonset Point, Rhode Island." We were constantly going to sea for training and our home comings were like repeated Honey Moons as many of the pilots were fairly newly married. Our ward room chats indicated many tricks to get the kids out of the house for a while upon our return to port. One pilot said he always had a bag of green Jelly Beans that he would throw out on the grass and tell the kids to find them. Another said he threw a handful of dimes and told the kids there were five quarters, which didn't exist, among the dimes.

Training for future Command is a prime concern for Officers and therefore it was a practice in VS 24 to rotate the Junior Officers every six months into a new assignment. such as the Metal Shop, the Electrical Shop, Electronics Shop, Ordnance, Personnel, Administration, the Line Crew that washed, fueled, and cared for the aircraft on the Flight Line, and Mechanics. This practice also applied to our Operational Training so that the squadron officers, destroyer officers, and submarine officers could learn the tactics and tricks of the air, sea, and sub-surface. We would cross train by spending a few days in the others realm. I had the good fortune to spend time on the USS QUILLBACK, which was a battery driven snorkel type submarine. Once below the surface there is no water motion to move the vessel about. It is "Run Silent, Run Deep" atmosphere. We could hear the aircraft flying over head and also the noise from the carrier and destroyers. Bunk beds had little vertical separation and if you rolled on your side you might just contact the bottom of the bunk above with your hip. The skipper permitted me to view the propellers of the carrier through the periscope and then sent a message to the Task Group Commander that he had sunk the ship by shooting off a green flare. "Wise Guy!!!!"

During these "Cold War" times we would occasionally locate one of Russia's submarines loitering off the East Coast and would attempt to track his underwater movement for a short time. The Korean War was in progress during this time frame, however there was no submarine problem in Korea and I never was involved in that conflict.

In January of 1954 we embarked aboard the USS LEYTE, CVS 32 for a return training mission to the Guantanamo Bay area. This time we were aboard the first WWII sized carriers that had been redesignated for use in the ASW mission The deck was huge, compared to the CVE and CVL carriers we had been flying from. At the cut we were picking and choosing our wire. Finally one of the pilots floated into the number seven cable and nicked the propeller on the barrier wires. That ended our delayed landings and the Skipper was furious. The blue flavored words were, "Land the G– D---- airplane!!!"

One memorable event that would never exist in today's world of Political Correctness is worthy of mention in this BIO. We had been at sea for two weeks with very little flying due to rough weather and heavy seas. On the final day of the session it was decided to launch all the aircraft into the wind off of the catapult on the upswing of the deck. All the aircraft had been securely tied down with nine point ties. (3 cables on each wheel). We maned the planes, warmed the engines prior to turning into the waves. It was, "Scary" as the ship rolled to starboard and port you were looking down at the water, or down at the plane parked on the opposite side. My Gyro Horizon indicated 22 degrees of roll. No way could the planes be untied. The ship finally turned into the wind and we were launched on the upswing of the deck. Twelve planes headed for feet dry off the coast of Atlantic City. The CO made contact and filed a flight plan for Quonset Pt. About 30 miles from home base he called the Tower for a landing for 12 aircraft. The tower informed us that the field was on instruments and we would have to break up and individually climb and hold on the South East Leg of the Quonset Radio Range. His reply was, "Clear the runways we are 12 AFs coming in VFR for landing. We alit on any available runway and taxied into our parking area. If anything like that would happen today the CO would be relieved and probably passed over for any promotion. Our Navy of today is so full of Politically Correct culture and fear of promotion that the officers are afraid of their shadows

On one particular night hop of note, it was decided that we would launch 12 aircraft for what was called a Group Grope. The planes were to return to ship at a certain time, join up into three 4 plane divisions and fly around the carrier force prior to breaking up and landing. The briefing was confused and each division leader was to flash a code letter on the upper signal light, such as an A, C, or D so that the wing men would know who to join on. It was completely confused and the signal to man planes left us all in a dither. The squadron always designated a full Lieutenant as flight deck expeditor. My aircraft was parked forward, just aft the Starboard Catapult. I noticed the parachute D Ring was hanging down about 10 inches into my lap. This indicated that the release pins in the chute may be on the edge of popping out. I signaled the bridge that I had a need for a new chute.The expeditor, Lt. Talbot tried to shove the D ring into the webbing and I refused to take the chute. The launch was delayed and I got out on the wing and pulled the chute to give it off to maintenance. I thought if that chute billows it will pull the man into the prop behind me. I shut down the engine. A new chute was provided and I restarted and launched. Upon return to the carrier the Squadron Duty Officer pulled me aside and said, "The Skipper is livid, you had better head for the double bottoms!!! I noticed the parachute lying on the deck in the ready room and took my seat. The Commanding Officer arrived and proceeded to start chewing out individuals one after the other, such as, "Yount, your lights were on flashing instead of bright and steady!! Blackwell your hook wasn't down and caused a wave off!! Strader your flaps weren't fully down!!! and finally "SCHAER, You can tell your grand children you held up an entire carrier task force for 25 minutes while you fiddle f–ed around with a G–D parachute!!! Get out of my sight!!!"

Six years later that skipper was the Commanding Officer of the Naval Air Station Norfolk. Tim Yount and I called on him to say Hello. We had a very enjoyable time and he explained that the Admiral was chewing on him for every possible reason the entire time of the flight. He had examined the chute and would not have taken off with it himself. He said that it was the funniest experience of his entire Naval Career.

We had almost three years of New England Weather and I informed the family we very probably would be transferred to warm, sunny, beautiful, Pensacola for Instructor Duty. To my chagrin we moved to the POOPY BAG station at Naval Air Station Lakehurst, New Jersey. I was to be the new Personnel Officer. I was informed the position was vacated by promotion and that I was selected from five photos of Lieutenants Junior Grade who were available for shore duty. We occupied Quarters on the base and even a burned out light bulb was replaced by Public Works. There were only a few Heavier than Air pilots aboard and I maintained my flight proficiency in several planes I had never flown before. The permanent Operations Duty Officer was a Chief Warrant Officer, Patrick Burns, I found out that he had been promoted to Lieutenant Commander during WWII and after the war was forced to return to his Warrant Officer status. He was very bitter about that. I thought I was a HOT SHOT carrier pilot with 148 carrier landings to my record and asked him one day if he had every landed aboard a carrier. "Matey, I landed on the Langley when two sand bags tied to a rope were the arresting cables!!!" Shut my mouth!!!He had been on loan from the Navy to Pan American Airways when they were setting up the sea ways for their water landing sites off the East Coast and Rio De Janeiro. He had over 27,000 flight hours. He was awarded the Legion Of Merit by the Secretary of the Navy upon his retirement. I flew several hops with him in the SNB and he always jumped into the left seat. As we were rolling on the runway for take off he was leaning out the mixture controls to save fuel. He comment was, "You never know when you may need that extra gallon!!" He bragged that he was the only ferry pilot that could take the PBY aircraft from San Diego to the East Coast with only one fuel stop. He pointed out a filling station on the ground one day and said, " I used to land in that field and sleep in the back room of that station when I was ferrying planes across country. The owner only charged 50 cents for the night. I never spent one cent of my flight pay. I saved it for my children." The line crew knew he was very conservative and one day placed a scrap of soap on the pathway. He picked it up and showed it to them and said, "Many a hand washing left in that piece of soap, Mates!!"

Several items of interest are of note: During construction start up of the Catapult and Arresting Gear installation in 1955 the Bull Dozer Operators were uncovering ammunition and were refusing to continue their work.. I had moved from Personnel Officer to Ordnance Officer and called in an Explosive Ordnance Demolition team to clear the site. It was reported that the Russians had used that area in the 1911 time frame for an firing range. The town of Lakewood, New Jersey has several buildings of Russian Design. The team dug up several large piles of unexploded projectiles and Livens Gas Bombs which were detonated so that construction could continue.

During Fleet introduction of the F4U Corsair fighter plane during WWII there were numerous pilot deaths during diving runs in which the planes dove into the ground. Control reversal was discovered when a pilot tried to pull back on the stick and the aircraft tucked under into a steeper dive. He pushed the stick forward and the plane recovered. This story was told to me by that pilot, Commander Beacham, who was the Operations Officer.

The Station had a DC3 (R4D Navy Designation) and it was primarily flown by a Chief Petty Officer Enlisted Pilot who had 17,000 flight hours. I flew several trips as Co-Pilot with the Chief. We stopped at an Air Force Base to refuel and got a snack at the Base Exchange. There were no seats, just stand up tables. I said, "Wonder why they don't have seats?" The Chief dryly responded, "That's the only way they can get the Air Force Jerks off their asses!!!"

The actual town of Lakehurst was very small. It had the normal village idiot that walked around town with a twisted baseball cap, his tongue sticking out of the side of his mouth, and was tossing a ball up and catching it all day long. We stopped for an Ice Cream cone and the proprietor lifted the cat off the counter and filled the cones without washing his hands. Billie and I walked out of a Bowling Alley in Toms River one Sunday afternoon and saw the most beautiful 1956 Lavender Lincoln Premier. She called the dealer in Camden the next day and he told her that he would take in our trade at twice the value we had previously been offered and put us behind the wheel of a Four Door Sedan for only $3700 dollars. We test drove the car and returned to our Quarters on the base leaving the car parked across the road from the house, (no garage). The Lincoln was painted Huntsman Red with a Black roof and White Leather seats. The Commanders and Captain of the base were aghast at a Lieutenant Junior Grade driving a beautiful Lincoln Continental. The Captain stopped me on the stairs and asked how I could afford such a car. I calmly replied that Billie's family had several producing Oil Wells in Texas. A fib, but it gave me great satisfaction because the base was a hornets nest of gossiping Commanders wives who looked down on Junior Officers and enlisted personnel. I was promoted to Lieutenant in May of 56, our family had grown to three boys. Mark born at Quonset Pt. and Matt born at Lakehurst. We were more than ready to leave the Blimps to their own. By the way, originally airship pilots uniform insignia was a Half Wing. In the early 50's they were given basic airplane instruction and from then on had the full Gold Wings.

BACK TO SCHOOL

On leave traveling to Naval Officer's Line School at Monterey, CA we stopped and visited our respective parents in Columbus, Ohio and Corpus Christi, Texas. My "Old School" mother had softened a bit and we had a short but pleasant visit. Billie's parents were more compatible. We stopped at all the tourist sites on the trip. Billie later said she never got to see half the scenery as she was busy changing diapers and feeding kids. The Line School curriculum was designed to acquaint non Naval Academy Officers with courses that were taught at the Naval Academy. Monterey allowed us to visit San Francisco, the Mystery Spot at Santa Cruz, Yosemite Redwoods, and all that California had to offer within weekend driving distance. The training was nine months duration and it was well organized so that the wives could take up activities in the evenings leaving the dads to baby sit and study. I was a whiz at Math and helped several friends with the Algebra problems. One in particular was an enthusiastic comic who entertained at any opportunity. Billie had organized a bowling awards ceremony consisting of about 400 persons. We had attended small groups of Friday night get togethers where I had sung along with the crowd. I was a bit bashful to speak to large audiences and up to this point had no reason to do so. The "Comic" explained that he had to get ready to do one of his acts and needed time to change into a costume and that I was to entertain the crowd with my rendition of "The Hole In The Bottom of the Sea". He grabbed the mike and announced that "MO Schaer, the flower of the Mathematical World", was going to lead us in a song. I was shoved into the lime light and left my shyness behind me. Lesson learned!!!

After line school, five of us were ordered to Electronics Officer's School of 40 weeks duration at the Naval Air Station, Memphis, TN. We were taught basic electronics and then acquainted with the special circuits involved in every black box in naval aircraft. The primary purpose of the school was "Advantages of Preventative Maintenance." We were to return to the fleet and improve the operation of the black boxes. This was prior to the explosion in transistors and micro circuits. The instructor drew a piece of Swiss cheese on the black board and explained that some how electrons could flow through the holes. "That's all we know about Transistors at this time. That's it, Back to Tubes." We maintained our flying proficiency by exploring the Mississippi River and occasionally a cross county in the T28 and T 34 training planes. My one and only experience with St. Elmo's fire took place at night in a thunderstorm on our way into Norfolk. The turbulence was intense and the propeller was encased in a purplish hue, noise in our earphones like a turbine coming up to speed and an orange ball, the size of a basketball, was bouncing on our right wing tip and slowly worked it's way toward the propeller which suddenly flashed bright white and then darkness. We were flipped completely over. We recovered control and had lost all electrical systems. Fortunately within a few minutes we broke out in the clear, spotted the lights along the Chesapeake Bay, circled down through the clouds and found the beacon from the Navy airfield. A low pass by the tower gave us a green light for landing. We opened the under belly hatch for our duffle bags and several gallons of water gushed out. We both recalled our pre-flight instructors warning, "Never fly into a thunderstorm if you can avoid it."

My class mate and cohort on that trip was "Smokey" Stovall. We had been in the same class during basic training. He and another pilot had been involved in a program to land a fully loaded C130 four engine aircraft aboard a Navy Carrier at sea. No tail hooks and no catapult. The mission was proven to be feasible.

We resided on the south east side of Memphis and Mike attended the Harding Academy of Memphis (HAM) which at that time was from 1st though 6th grades. The school was affiliated with the Church of Christ. It was housed in the Wrigley family Estate. Memphis was still in the throes of racist and Confederate bigotry. Since we had been stationed in New England, New Jersey and California Mike was ordered to the back of the school bus by the driver for being a YANKEE!! When he reported this to Mom all hell broke loose!! She sought out the driver, grabbed her by the hair and in no uncertain terms told her she would jerk her hair out if that ever happened again. School Administration was apologetic and the air returned to it's natural brilliance. We followed the growth of the school with contributions over the years and were told that the athletic teams were referred to as HAMS. The name has changed. It is now listed on the map as the Harding University Graduate School of Religion. In August 1958, Mo, Mom, Mike, Mark and Matt proceeded to Norfolk, VA for more adventure.

BACK TO SEA DUTY

We had several weeks of leave for leisure prior to reporting for duty with Air Anti-Submarine Squadron TWENTY SEVEN. We opted to purchase a home under construction in a new development named Poplar Halls off Military Highway in Norfolk. This was in the midst of school integration and the schools had not yet opened for the year. We rented a beach house and had access to a rowboat the boys could play with. Billie and I constructed a treasure map, burned the edges of the paper and hid it under the bath tub. Naturally it was discovered and the pirates treasure four paces north from a lone tree on the island across the inlet from our house kept the boys awake to the wee hours. First thing in the morning we maned the oars and set out for the treasure which I had hidden the day before while Billie took the boys shopping for school clothes. It was several months before they realized Mom and Dad had fooled them. We had a great few weeks living by the water with all the fishing and excitement that goes with an old beach house and an approaching hurricane that passed without serious damage. Construction of the home was finally completed, schools had opened and I reported for duty.

The two single engine ASW aircraft, AF and TBM, had been replaced with the Grumman S2 Tracker, a twin engine carrier plane with Pilot, Co-Pilot, and two electronic equipment operators. The earlier practice of giving a newly reporting pilot a handbook for the aircraft, time to read it over, and telling him to go fly was over. The Navy had established Naval Air Maintenance Training Detachments (NAMTRADETS) and classroom instruction concerning all the aircraft systems and electronic equipment was thoroughly explained and taught. Several weeks of this ground school and the newcomer returned to the squadron for familiarization flights with an experience pilot to acquaint the member with the local flying area, regulations, practice targets and touch and go landings. Every other hop from then on was the left seat. You were a member of the team. The smaller deck carriers had been replaced with the larger WWII carriers designated specifically for the Anti-Submarine role, (CVS), the "C" for carrier, "V" for heavier than air, and "S" for Anti-Submarine. Names such as LEYTE, VALLEY FORGE, LAKE CHAMPLAIN, TARAWA were the carriers used with the Atlantic Fleet. Our constant training and surveillance involved alternating periods ashore and at sea. Exercises were set up so that the submarine and ASW Task Group would have to operate in a several hundred mile long rectangular area. We tried to find the sub and the sub tried to attack the carrier. This game of cat and mouse lasted for two to three weeks at a time. Sometimes the sub won and sometimes the destroyers and planes won. The time frame was 1959/60 and the "Cold War" was in progress. Occasionally we would detect a Russian sub operating off the east coast and would play cat and mouse for a day or two.

My training in Electronics was put to use by the CO and I was assigned as Avionics Officer. The Navy had organized a group of Electronic Technicians to assist the Fleet. Naval Aviation Electronics Service Unit

(NAESU) was available in the Atlantic and Pacific Fleet for this purpose. These technicians would be assigned to the requesting squadron and would guide and assist the squadron personnel in the repair and tune up of the various equipments. The poorest working system was the Magnetic Anomaly Detector (MAD). This unit extended from the tail of the plane and contained a soft iron core that could be magnetically aligned with the earth lines of magnetic flux. It operated from a low sensitivity of 1, to perfect at sense 10. Our equipment was in the low range. As the aircraft flew over the ocean at about 300 feet any magnetic body such as a submarine or sunken ship or ore deposit could cause a deflection on the graph in the aircraft. The operator knew that if the water was deeper than the max range of the equipment it must be a submarine. I assigned four technicians to work under the guidance of the NAESU Rep. In about five months of tedious repair and adjustment and refinement that crew attained sense 10 operation on every plane in the squadron. The Commanding Officer was publically commended for being the only Squadron, East and West Coast, to achieve that goal. This effort enthused the Avionic Crew to look into other systems. Soon the pilots were reporting that they could see all the metal buoys in the ship channels of the bay which had never shown up before on their radar. The crew assigned to the underwater noise detection receivers made vast improvements that were acknowledge by the manufacturer of the buoys. The Schooling at Memphis had far reaching results in the fleet. Equipment that had been dubbed as" FAIR" was now considered "GREAT".

In addition to the VS Squadron planes, our task group contained a helicopter ASW Squadron and a four plane detachment of the AD5N, Sky Raider, early warning aircraft. The AD engine was a Wright Cyclone 3350 radial engine that generated a large amount of torque under high power settings. On take off from a runway or carrier deck it was necessary to add throttle carefully with right rudder so that the torque would not carry you off to the left. A newly reported pilot into the detachment was given the two finger turn up for a deck launch and applied full throttle too rapidly. The aircraft rolled to the left and the left wheel fell off into the port catwalk, broke off the plane on the rear edge of the deck edge elevator, skidded across the steel elevator while slicing 28 nine inch gashes completely through the steel decking, and disappeared below flight level. We thought he had crashed when the plane came climbing upward and gained altitude. The pilot radioed for an immediate landing and was fearful that the severely vibrating engine would break off the fuselage. He was ordered to continue climbing out and head west to Oceana, VA and that another plane would accompany him to shore which was 120 miles to the west. He was begging the Operations Officer to ditch along side the carrier and was screaming that the engine was going to break off. "Be Calm, head west to Oceana, that's an ORDER!!" About sixty miles from shore he wanted to ditch alongside the USS Galveston and again was ordered to continue to the beach. He landed safely on a foamed runway at Oceana!!! The AD Sky Raider could carry 10,000 pounds of bombs which was equivalent to the load of the Boeing B17 during WWII.

While deployed off the east coast and in the Gulf Stream a four plane flight was launched for Rocket Firing practice. The target was a long wooden spar being towed behind the carrier. We were loaded with six 5 inch inert steel headed rockets. The rockets were going in all directions as they left the rail. The Skipper called for cease fire, and requested to fly the malfunctioning ordnance into the shore base. Orders were to go off into a ship free area and fire them off the wings. One of the planes lost an engine. I flew along side and reported that the plastic dome on the right wing searchlight was missing. Apparently one of the rockets left the rail and flew immediately into the searchlight dome. It was conjectured that another had damaged the right engine. All four planes expended the defective ordnance. Several days prior to the hop we had been discussing single engine carrier landings and the two pilots flying that particular plane had stated emphatically, "If I couldn't land an S2 single engine, I'd turn in my wings!!" Those two pilots were in that plane. Both were experience pilots, one a Lieutenant Commander and the other a full Commander with many flight hours. Coming aboard the carrier with the single engine the plane stalled out just aft the stern of the carrier and crashed into the sea. Neither pilot was recovered, the two aircrewmen survived. An investigation into the rocket malfunction revealed that a 3/4 inch hole had been drilled into the nose of the hollow steel head and the plug that should have been screwed into the bottom of the head was never installed. The gases from the propellant blew into the head and out the 3/4 hole acting like a thruster to turn the rocket away from the exhaust. The Yorktown Arsenal had supplied the rockets to the carrier and the Ordnance men did not notice a problem. An unfortunate accident snuffed two lives!!!!

Carrier pilots have two signals they must obey from the Landing Signal Officer. The "CUT" and the "WAVE OFF." No questions, "DO IT." My Co-Pilot and I had launched for a test flight that required a full in flight shut down of the starboard engine with a restart to check the propellor feathering system. We completed the test and noticed a fluttering in the rudder pedals which was abnormal. The regular launch of four planes was due back at the ship within a few minute and the carrier had turned into the wind. We reported the problem and asked for a straight in prior to the four plane recovery.It was granted and just as we were in position for a CUT the LSO waved us off. The tail hook caught the number two wire and I had applied full throttle for the wave off. We were slammed down onto the left main mount and the left wing tip hit the deck and also the left prop. We almost went over the port side. The LSO ran up to the plane and hollared, "MO!!! My mind said CUT and my hands WAVED OFF". Fortunately for me, the accident was observed by the Admiral, the Squadron CO and the ships Operations Officer. I was exonerated!! That is one of a very few flight deck accidents non-attributed to PILOT ERROR.

Between these short two to three week at sea periods our wives were busy with their children and squadron wives gatherings. The camaraderie of Navy families is sorely missed after retiring from the Naval Service. Our wives knew the importance of our jobs and the husbands knew the importance of their wives. Many green jelly beans and coins were thrown on the lawns!!! From January 1960 through April we were on and off the USS Valley Forge. The ship had been tasked to launch a balloon from the vicinity of Puerto Rico. The squadron off loaded at the Naval Air Station Roosevelt Roads while the carrier completed its task. We flew local hops, played a little golf and visited several small towns including San Juan while awaiting the availability of the carrier. The Flight Surgeon warned about reaching into or wading in the streams around the golf course to fetch a golf ball as the water contained a harmful parasite that could penetrate the skin and work it's way into the internal organs. My golf balls seemed to head into the water and I let them rest in peace. We returned to the comfort of the carrier and took up our game of cat and mouse. This training cruise offered visits to St. Thomas and St. Croix and the wonderful Steel Band Music. While relaxing with a few drinks at the "Black Patch" the owner explained he was going broke before Time Magazine wrote an article about the islands of the Caribbean, and mentioned the "Black Patch." From that time on every cruise ship filled his bar with customers. He was doing a roaring business.

We returned to Norfolk on 18 May 1960. Billie was expecting in July and we were scheduled to depart for the Mediterranean in early June. Normal pregnancy is not considered an emergency. We decided it would be best if Grandma came to Norfolk to be with Mom and the boys

During this short in port period Air Anti-Submarine Squadron TWENTY FOUR which had been disbanded earlier with the AF aircraft was being Re-Commissioned with some of the VS 27 planes and personnel. Commander Robert Eslinger who had been in the Quonset Squadron and myself were to be the first two members of the newly Commissioned Squadron. He was the Commanding Officer and I was the Maintenance Officer. We departed Norfolk on 9 June aboard USS VALLEY FORGE. Our first port of call was at CADIZ, Spain to off load one F-11F Tiger Cat to be transported to Naval Air Station, ROTA. I was flown in to arrange the off load and transfer. I took a bus ride from Rota to Cadiz. The sun was shining and the air was clear, I suddenly smelled the odor of garbage, looked up and we were passing through a small village. This happened several times. That evening while strolling along the sidewalks I noticed the men and boys would just urinate against the front of the stores. My father was born in Switzerland and entered the United States in 1910. My mother used to ask if he every yearned to go back home. His reply was, "Europe is decayed. Those beautiful photos that you see of Castles along the Rhine do not show you the broken hinges, the rotten floors and holes in the walls. I never want to go home. Every one is in a secret organization!! Any thing that Europe has is 50 times better in the United States!!!!!" The plane was off loaded and delivered and we began the game of cat and mouse in the Mediterranean Sea.

Mell was born in Norfolk on July 21,1960 and I was notified aboard ship somewhere in the Med that he had arrived safely and Mom and son were doing fine. We were now the six M's: Mommy, Mo, Mike, Mark, Matt and Mell.

During June and July we visited the beaches at Cannes and Nice, France; La Spezia, Italy where the merchandise items are bolts of fine materials and fancy umbrellas; flew over the Leaning Tower of Pisa; anchored off Naples and visited the ruins of Pompeii; watched the craftsmen carving Cameo Pins from sea shells; attended a Bull Fight in Barcelona and viewed a fantastic stage production with full flowing skirts, castanets and Flamenco Dancing; visited Palma on the island of Mallorca, a vacation spot for the Europeans; and made a final stop at Gibraltar on the way back to the Greatest Country in the World. In Barcelona the women would come down from tall, bare, concrete buildings with a jug to get a little water from a pipe bubbling up in the middle of the street. As the dew started settling on the streets at night the entire area smelled of urine. Once you penetrated the tourist area and went into the back streets you were in a jungle. Decrepit old bare rooms, crowded with people living in one room and sleeping on the floor. There is no place like the United States of America. Even in our smallest, run down town, you can get a good drink of water.

We arrived in Norfolk at the end of August and I soon received orders to the USS KITTY HAWK, a newly constructed large deck carrier for "On Board Commissioning and Outfitting." At this time the Commanding Officer had received notice that experienced pilots were needed to train the Brazilian Air Force with Operation, Maintenance and Anti-submarine Warfare Tactics at the Naval Air Station in Key West, FL. The orders were changed to Key West. I was delighted as "Ships Company" aboard a carrier meant long and numerous separations from the family. I had been warned by several ships officers I had met, that you never see your wife and kids, and to avoid those orders if at all possible.

SHORE DUTY

The military wanted a missile tracking station in north east Brazil to monitor shots from Cape Canaveral. An agreement was reached to establish an Anti-Submarine Task Force in the South Atlantic Ocean for permission to set up and operate the tracking station. The Carrier was provided by the British, it was to be overhauled in the Netherlands and manned by Brazilian Navy. The Brazilian Air Force was to be provided with the S2 Tracker Aircraft, and ASW Helicopters. Training for the Air Force to be in Key West. The "Brazilian Mobile Training Team" consisted of 12 Officers and 50 experienced maintenance men. Brazilian Air Force Personnel (30 Pilots and 360 men) and many of their wives arrived in February. The newly manufactured aircraft arrived on 2 March and we were off and running. Our training went well primarily because many of the Brazilian Officers had received flight training and other specialized schooling in the United States and spoke excellent English. My counterpart had in fact, married a young lady from his flight training days in Milton, Florida. They had been told not to work on the weekends but to take every opportunity to see the United States. We had one glitch when the only Submarine availability was over a week end. It was take the training with a submarine or never get another chance. They took it!! Friday evening at the Officers Club was Mardi Gras Time. They brought all their toots and whistles and swept our wives off their feet with dancing and good times. My good friend, along with Mike (15 yrs), caught four large Bull Dolphin on a deep sea fishing trip. We fed 60 persons from those four fish at one of the TGIF affairs. They were all seeking nice used cars to take home on the carrier. A 57 Chevy was reported to be worth $13,000 in Rio. As the last weeks of training were counting down the sad news came that the carrier would not be coming to take on their goodies. It was a hectic time for them to try and sell their washers and dryers and used cars. I'm sure the Key West residents took advantage of their misfortune. Two American Officers returned to Brazil with the group to assist and provide guidance until they were operating up to speed. The carrier crew was Navy, the planes were Air Force. I was told later that the Air Force Officers went aboard the ship. They gathered in the Ward Room to discuss air operations and were told that the ship would be scheduling their flights as is done in the US Navy. An "Impasse!!!" They stared at each other for two hours, walked off and never flew onto the carrier for two years. My cohort wrote that they took great photos of the annual yacht races from Newport to Rio.

An interesting side line to the Key West duty. Housing in the Keys is limited and we were unable to move into the house we found for rent until that officer moved out. A month of living in the Hibiscus Motel with a pool was delightful for the family. This was the time of Castro's taking over. We were dining at Logan Lobster House when the last ferry boat departed for Havana. Word was out to watch your children as kidnappings were possible. President Kennedy and the Prime Minister of England landed at the base for a conference. Sailors in Dress Whites were lined up every ten feet for the quarter mile ride to the exit of the station. The Blue Angles were in the same hanger we had for the Brazilians and the kids and the Brazilians got to talk to and meet the pilots. Key West is a fisherman's paradise and Mike Mark and Matt caught large fish. I had parked the car at the foot of the seven mile bridge one Sunday afternoon.. Mell's stroller was in the trunk, We got out, I gave the boys their rods and while taking the stroller out they were all yelling. DAD!!, DAD !!, Mike had hooked a four foot Hammer Head baby shark, Mark had hooked a four foot Sting Ray, and Matt's rod was arched with a blow fish that had expanded between two rocks and couldn't be pulled out. A stranger came to the rescue, warned us that the spikes were poisonous, do not touch, and released the blow fish into the water. After Key West the boys had no further yens to catch a five inch long Blue Gill. I never recall any of them wanting to go fishing after Key West. Mell was entered in the annual Baby Contest and won a Blue Ribbon for Beautiful Baby. Key West was truly a wonderful tour of duty for the entire family after the long separations with VS27 and VS 24.

FIVE TERM PROGRAM

The Brazilians flew off and we motored in two cars headed for Monterey, CA and schooling for a College Degree. We spent two weeks in Corpus Christi visiting Billie's family, stopped at all the tourist sights along the road, such as Judge Roy Bean's Law Office, Painted Desert, Grand Canyon, Death Valley, Big Sur, Pebble Beach and purchased a home close to the Post Graduate School which is housed in the Pre-WWII Del Monte Hotel. At Check In, the review of my Ohio State Transcript provided ample credit to earn a Bachelor Of Science with a Major in Mathematics within one year. Having been away from math for more than 12 years our first refresher course was advanced Algebra. The Professor was quite jealous that we Naval Officers were receiving full pay for attending college and was determined that he would not be too helpful. "I had to work my way through college, you will just have to burn the mid-night oil!!!" He would write across the black board with his right hand while erasing behind with his left hand. We voiced concern that it was impossible to take notes in this manner. "You will just have to write faster!!" Half of the 30 student class were Naval Academy Graduates who were to earn a Masters in Operation Development, a Navy Warfare course. The cantankerous Professor passed out primarily C's and D's, which I was told later, prevented those officers from attaining a Masters. There are nasty people in every level of society!!! A friendly jest among we officers was that the Naval Academy was referred to as "Canoe U".

Monterey, Pebble Beach, Carmel and Big Sur is a beautiful, relaxing, area of this wonderful country. Again, the wives were organized into all types of activities and hobbies to socialize, while the hubbies did their home work and supervised the children. On weekends we visited all the points of interest within several hundred miles. San Francisco's China Town, the Golden Gate, excursion boat around Alcatraz Prison, San Jose, Stanford University, Santa Cruz Mystery Spot, where the boys had a great time, and the Famous Fisherman's Wharf area. There were many TGIF parties. One in particular included the Navy Warrant Officer and his wife who were the subjects of "Cheaper By the Dozen" movie. His wife had died, and her husband had been killed. They united with a total of 20 children. The merchants in Monterey provided shoes, clothing and groceries on several occasions to assist in their support of all the kids. He was an expert at "Cum Shaw" which is a Navy Term for making use of no longer needed items. His home had large cooking vats, convey belts, washers and dryers, pots and pans, etc. Each younger child was looked after by an older child. All the children had assigned tasks and his wife said she was very comfortable with the arrangement.

I had been promoted to Lieutenant Commander and with several other newly promoted Officers we arranged a "Wetting Down Party" at the Casa Munras Motel in Monterey. The annual Pebble Beach Golf Tournament was in session and Billie had called the hotel in which James Garner was staying to say, Hello, and to chat about their childhood watermelon escapades in Norman, Ok in their early teen years. He met us at the Party that evening and since it was raining, mentioned that we had picked a good night for a "Wetting Down." All the wives were agog at Billie and he chatting merrily about their childhood escapes from the constable. He said, "I knew it was from someone in Norman when you asked for James Bumgarner, normally I don't take a call." He left after a few minutes and Billie was busy the rest of the evening telling all about their childhood in Norman, OK.

We purchased a used Metallic Blue Cadillac with the "Bullet Tail Lights" from another Naval Officer. Billie was driving in heavy traffic in Monterey when the car stalled out in the center of the highway. She narrowly got to the side of the road without getting hit. Upon inspection the gas gage indicated 1/4 tank but the car was out of gas. I queried the Officer as to why he had not mentioned the needed repair and pointed out the danger he had laid on my wife. His response, "I just wanted to sell the car." Another NASTY person!!!

Computers were on the way into our lives and the main computer at the school was about 30 feet long and seven foot in height. We were required to write an amortization table for a home mortgage, type up the IBM Cards and submit it to the operators for insertion in the card readers. If the program ran we received credit for the course. At Graduation I had received orders to the Pentagon in the Chief of Naval Operations Organization, "Plans and Programs". I was elated that I would be able to work into this new field of computers making good use of mathematics and programming.

I had accrued plenty of leave and we decided that we would buy some camping equipment and take the boys across country like the pioneers. We purchased a small 4 X 4 foot, one swivel wheel trailer to tow behind the

Cadillac. Billie was to take Mike the eldest, and Mell the youngest, in the air conditioned auto and I would follow in the Lincoln with Mark and Matt. This worked out very nicely, we camped at Lake Tahoe the first night and other than getting very cold during the night it was fun! One of my former squadron mates had been killed in a plane crash and we planned a visit with his wife and mother in Pocatello, Idaho to help ease their suffering. We were going to Yellowstone the next day. I had the AAA maps depicting the route. The brother told us a much more, " Scenic" route was available and laid it out for the trip. Wonderful!!! We crossed the Wyoming State line and the road was under construction for the next twenty or more miles. It dropped off the nice paved road about six inches onto dirt and chuck holes. The one wheel trailer had a shock absorber that was ruined within just a short distance. When we got back on the paved road after 30 miles of rubble the wheel on the trailer would shimmy at over 20 miles per hour. Billie was following me as we crept along. We started the climb in the Tetons and the Lincoln started to get hot. The crest was not too distant and no water anywhere. I waved to Billie and went speeding up to the 8391 foot crest. Billie arrived about ten minutes later and I had the hood up and the car was cooling. I said, "The engine got hot and I had to get up here quick!!!" The typical "Navy Wife", who is the Commanding Officer of the household during Dad's absences, came back with, "THAT's NOT THE ONLY THING THAT's HOT." We all cooled off during the next half hour and then coasted down into Jackson Hole, Wyoming and spent the night in a Motel. So much for camping like the Pioneers!!!

Old Faithful was still on it's routine time schedule of every 90 minutes between eruptions but a recent earthquake had evidently shifted the land so that it no longer shot straight up as before. We rented a cabin for the night and heard the bears scratching at the walls searching for food. The boys had a nice experience at the Park and we left on a southerly direction to visit Billie's sister, Louise, in Dallas, TX. The 178 mile trip to Rock Springs took nine hours. We found a Sears Store and asked them to take the trailer and refund our account. The manager was not enthusiastic about taking in the trailer. After placing a Call to the Denver Sears Company the matter was settled and we unloaded the camping equipment at the nearest church. We visited the Air Force Academy, stopped at the Garden of the Gods for a horse back ride, rode the inclined train up Pikes Peak and then headed for Dallas.

BACK TO WORK

Louise and Paul welcomed our visit with open arms. Jimmy, Paul's son, and Mike hit it off and did their thing. Matt was not feeling well and Billie took him to the Air Station where he was diagnosed with Measles. Ordered to bed rest in a darkened room for eleven days. I extended my leave period to cover the illness and we all settled in for a longer than expected visit. Betty, Billie's cousin, and Arnold with their two children, Rajean and Ridge, and Rena, Billie's mother, drove up from Corpus Christi. The cousins all met for the first time and they had fun catching craw dads out of the stream and playing while Matt was in the darkened room. Recovery was normal with no complications and we departed "On The Road Again." We headed straight for Washington to search for a house prior to reporting for duty. Found a nice three story rental at 2500 Valley Drive in Alexandria. The house was built into the side of a hill with the Den level with the front yard, the first floor level with the back yard and bed rooms upstairs. Price was enormous at $195.00 per month. The previous tenant had painted the bedrooms deep red, deep blue and deep green. The CO(Billie) demanded repaint to neutral colors. "YES MA'AM." The furniture arrived, we set up house keeping, I went to the Pentagon and Billie enrolled the boys in school. We were ready for Washington.

My job was hectic and on the second day the Admiral asked if I played Hand Ball? I replied in the negative and when he left the office the Chief Petty Officer said, "You made the right answer because he doesn't go to the gym until 6 PM." It was usual for the Admirals to stay until the Secretary of the Navy left. The Captains stayed until the Admirals left, and I, as a Lieutenant Commander could leave at a normal hour. The Mathematics Degree and Computer programming, that I had hoped to expand, faded into just the numbers at the bottom of the written papers. No Computer Programming and no calculations were required of my assignment.

Our weekends were fully occupied for two years visiting all the wonderful sights located at the seat of our Government. Billie again was a Den Mother for the Cub Scouts. We took them to Ft. Meyers to the horse barn where all the Black and White Horses are stabled for Arlington Cemetery. The Sergeant told the Cubs about a particular horse, "Black Jack." If the Sergeant went out the barn door, and failed to close the top half of the horse stall, Black would reach over and unlatch the lower door. He would then go down the length of the barn talking to all the other horses. If the Sergeant stomped his feet the horse would trot back into his stall, swing the lower door back into place and act completely innocent. We all left the barn and watched. It happened as told!!!

We shopped at the Cameron Station Commissary Store and Lobster tails were very reasonably priced. We had been snacking on broiled tails while watching TV in the evenings. One afternoon, Matt who was 9 years old at the time, snuck up stairs to the kitchen to broil his own tail. It was a gas oven and evidently he turned on the gas and the first match went out before lighting. He lit the second match and the gas exploded into his face. His eyebrows were burnt off and he was screaming. We rushed up and ran him to the dispensary. Fortunately no damage to his eyes!!!He was a very active child and Billie had her hands full with the two youngest

An incident, that will appear again in this story, occurred on a Sunday outing at Rock Creek Park in Maryland. We were walking along the old Chesapeake and Ohio canal and I had Mell (only 3 yrs) along side. Billie said, "Be careful he doesn't fall in." I replied,"I'm watching him." PLOP!!!, Mell had stumble into the water and was face down with arms and legs fanned out about six inches below the surface!!! I jumped in and with my left arm snatched him onto the grass!! It was a cool day and we immediately drove home and scrubbed off. The canal was reported to be polluted and we were concerned he may become ill. He didn't. I received an earned tongue lashing over that fiasco. Moms' never forget!!! It will come back later!!!

My mother, Norma and Aunt Anna, mentioned earlier, all communicated with each other. I was told that my cousin Kenneth Bechtold, whom I had never met, was also in the Pentagon. We both resided in Alexandria and that summer Norma and Ruth, her room mate, visited Washington and we all had a family reunion. Kenneth was an Army Lieutenant Colonel.. After retirement the family settled in Roswell, New Mexico and he later passed away from a heart Attack.. Billie, Betty and Ginny were teenagers during WWII in Corpus and dated the flight cadets. All married Marine pilots in the 45/49 time frame. Ginny's husband, Jess Hall, had been recalled to active duty during the Korean War. After the war he was employed by the Navy and was a Mechanical Engineer with the Bureau of Naval Weapons in D.C.. We had many pleasant week end sight seeing trips together during our Washington duty.

Mike purchased his first car from Paper Route money that he saved. It was an old faded blue Plymouth and ran reasonably well for a few months. The engine finally went "KAPUT" and I recall that it was junked prior to our transfer. Mike had always been very reliable, from the age of 12 we never again hired a Baby Sitter. He took his task seriously and Mom and I felt more secure with his sitting than we did with others. To this point Mike had attended 16 schools, he was in the eleventh grade at Washington.

In November of 63 President Kennedy was assassinated in Dallas. Thousands assembled at the Capitol to view his body. Mike took the movie camera up on the roof of a building and photographed the caisson with "Black Jack" the horse passing with the boots facing to the rear. Those photos may be seen on the five VHS tapes your family was given in 1990. I had mentioned in the office that LBJ was somehow involved in Kennedy's assassination. The Captain working next to me said, "Mo, he is now our Commander-in-Chief, be careful what you say."

All in all the Washington tour of duty was a wonderful experience for the entire family. Our next assignment was back to the Pacific Fleet in the San Diego, CA locale. In preparation for another cross country trek we traded the 1959 Blue Bullet Tail Cadillac for a Black 1969 Suicide Door Lincoln. My date of transfer was August. In June, when school was out, we closed out the house, shipped the furniture to San Diego and Billie took the children to vacation in Corpus. I took up residence at Ft. Meyers Bachelor Officers Quarters. She stopped in Columbus to visit Grand mother and was not very cordially received. Still the "Old School" temperament that did not thaw until mother was on her death bed, which will be described later.

I departed in August for Corpus with a pass by my home. Mother and I had a long talk about accepting my wife and family. I laid down the law and for the next several years their was no communication. She was as hard headed as my father had been. Divorce in those days was looked down upon. "It must have been the woman's fault."

Billie's vacation with her family allowed the children to meet their cousins and get to know each other. Mike at this time was turning 18, Mark was 12, Matt was going on 10 and Mell had just turned 4. Cousins were Ridge aged 13 and sister Rajean age 10, on the Hammons family, and Mike Hames age 17. They had spent the summer, fishing, swimming and movies and were ready to hit the road for another adventure. We departed in the two car caravan and since we had taken this trip three years earlier by-passed many of the tourist sites. We did however visit Judge Roy Beans Office for the second time. Aunt Anna, in Tucson, had passed away but we stopped at Saguaro National Monument east of Tucson for pictures beside the tall cacti.

Arriving in San Diego, we purchased a 1400 sqft home at 10356 Strawberry Lane in Spring Valley, a suburb of San Diego for $17,100. Gasoline was in the 20 cent per gallon range. Inflation had not yet taken hold and pay checks were small. I had sufficient leave to set up house keeping and settle the family prior to checking into the new assignment.

SAN DIEGO

I checked into work, and with another Lieutenant Commander who had just check in, discovered that we were to be the Two Team Leaders to transition Navy Aircraft Maintenance to a data collection system originated in the Air Force and named Standard Navy Maintenance Management and Material System, abbreviated "SNMMMS" commonly called the 3M Program. Each team was composed of five top notch Chief Petty Officers. Our Task was to train all Naval Air Maintenance Personnel aboard Air Stations and Carriers in the entire Pacific Fleet to properly document on IBM Type Computer Input cards exactly what was needed to repair and maintain Naval aircraft and associated support equipments. The training at each location was about five days. I seldom saw Billie and my sons for more than two days every once in awhile. We worked our way across the Pacific to Japan and hit all the aircraft carriers and shore stations en route.

During my absence, Billie as most Navy (Military) Wives, took charge of the family and carried on in their husbands absence. Mike was working part time while finishing High School and had purchased a Triumph Sports Car. Mark and Matt were members of the Hickory Pit Soft Ball Team in Spring Valley and Mike taught them to slide into bases, which they did at every opportunity. Mell was entering school as a first grader. As the year 1965 progressed, Billie started Mark and Matt in Horse Back Riding lessons in Bonita Valley at the Bradley Riding Stable. Billie had a way with horses and soon was leading the pack on "Mr. Frank" which she had purchased for $150. The beginning of "Shoveling Manure and Hollering Whoa." Her reasoning was that if she kept the boys busy they would not be lured into the pot smoking and drug world which was becoming rampant among the school aged children. (I was told in later years that there WAS some pot smoking in the hay stacks at the stable during that time period.) Riding lessons turned to competing in week end horse shows primarily for Billie and Mark. They had worked their way up the ladder and were starting to win an occasional Blue Ribbon. Matt was an excellent rider and sat well on the horse but was not interested in the show circuit. My occasional week end at home visit, convinced me that a motorcycle was more to my liking than an unpredictable horse. Mike preferred his four wheels rather than four legs and little Mell was having trouble with a slight touch of dyslexia with regard to 4's and h's. Fortunately his school teacher was versed in the subject and worked with him to solve the problem.

This "Have bag will travel" odyssey came to an abrupt halt in May of 1966 when I was notified that I had been promoted to Commander and was to return to base for further orders. I had been screened for Squadron Command and was to report to Air Anti-Submarine Squadron 41, (VS41), based at Naval Air Station North Island as Executive Officer pending an opening in Air Anti-Submarine Squadron 33, (VS33), at a later date. Wonderful!!!, I would be home every night and get to see the wife and kids again. This assignment allowed me to feed Mr. Frank and clean out his stall while going to and from work at the North Island Naval Air Station. Mom had been running back and forth for that chore for over a year. VS41 was a Replacement Air Group, (RAG), Training Squadron and did not deploy at sea except to qualify the pilots in landing the S2 aircraft aboard the carrier. For 22 months until March of 1968 I was with my family on a daily basis. We visited all the sights in the southern California area such as Disney Land, Sea World, Tijuana for hair cuts and shopping, the desert, sledding and snow balling in the Lagunas and the beaches. The family blended into the neighborhood and enjoyed Friday night songfests and camaraderie with life long friends. Most of those friends have passed away at the time of this writing.

Mike had enlisted in the Naval Reserve in October 1967 and was undergoing BOOT Training at the Naval Station in San Diego. Another horse owner from the Los Angeles area and her daughter came down to the stable on week ends to work their horses. The young lady had her eye on Mike and was rather wild. Billie had the motherly instinct to recognize a bad situation and said, "Mo, that girl is out to get herself pregnant with Mike." My First Class Yeoman in VS41 had just been transferred to the enlisted personnel area for the Pacific Fleet. I called to see if we could get Mike out of the area. His answer was, "Which Destroyer do you want him on, the USS Kitty Hawk and six Destroyers are leaving Tuesday morning." I named no preference and he responded that Mike will be aboard the USS PRITCHET leaving Tuesday. Problem Solved!!!!

I transferred from VS41 to Executive Officer of VS33 in March of 1968. We were scheduled to depart in May for Viet Nam with the first port call at Pearl Harbor.

The USS PRITCHET had completed her 6 months tour and would be in Pearl at the same time. Another call to my friendly Yeoman and orders were issued for Mike to transfer off the PRITCHET onto the BENNINGTON and into VS38 the sister squadron. Meanwhile Billie and the boys flew to Honolulu and the entire family enjoyed a five day vacation while we were in port. Billie and boys flew home and could see the BENNINGTON heading out to sea as they took off from the airport heading east.

Our deployment included periods on the line broken by in port calls. Mike and I particularly enjoyed the Tokyo city tour finalized with a fantastic stage production in which the set was set ablaze on stage. Mike had been assigned to the ship Photo Lab and learned the basics of Photography which stood him in good stead after his return to the states. Since VS Squadrons are primarily anti-submarine seekers, our orders were to stay three miles off the shore line. "There are no Submarines in North Vietnam and if you get one bullet hole in an S2 Aircraft you will never see another promotion in this mans Navy. Congress will have my Stripes and I guarantee I will have yours." A stern WARNING from the Admiral!!! We conducted our assigned mission in the Gulf of Tonkin, visited numerous foreign ports and returned to San Diego in October of 1968. Mike had served a total of 13 months, all of which was in the Combat Zone and was given credit for two full years of service and released to inactive duty.

The on line periods in the Gulf of 30 to 40 days of around the clock operation were broken by in port calls for replenishment and repairs. The Officer's Club at Cubi Point was a unique spot for pilots. The Commanding Officer of the Station recognized that a place was needed for them to blow off steam and relax without interference. Only the west coast squadrons were being used for Vietnam. It was not unusual for a pilot to complain that out of two years he had spent only 52 days with his family. A favorite game was to nudge someone off balance sending him crashing to the deck with table and chairs flying and glasses breaking. A Catapult Shot was to seat the pilot in a roller chair and shove him violently off a three step level into a tank of water. If he crossed a certain line his name and squadron were etched on a brass plate for eternity. The Catapult shot recognition board with all the brass plates was sent to the Pensacola Museum and may be seen there. All squadrons collected money for damages and sent it to the Club for replenishment of broken equipment. No interference from outsiders was allowed. It was all men and all fun and it was sorely needed after a rigorous period on line with Surface to Air Missiles (SAMS) and stormy night landings with low fuel state. Toward the end of the war east coast squadrons were finally engaged in the war. At one point 60 pilots turned in their wings in protest to the repetitive returns to the conflict while the east coast was never used. Several sea stories are interesting and occurred while conducting Surface, Sub-Surface, Surveillance throughout the Gulf of Tonkin.

The pilots of the two VS Squadrons maintained 24 hour around the clock surveillance of the Gulf. During a daylight search we encountered a beautiful water spout glistening in the sun as a latticework of rain streaks from the surface to 1500 feet. My co-pilot said, "Shall we fly through it?" My answer, "Let's not f–k with Mother Nature!! A B52 had it's wing torn off in Biggs, Texas by a funnel cloud." Evidently our two crewmen were pleased with my response and relayed it to their squadron mates. The next day as I was walking through the planes on the hanger deck, I heard two mechanics say, "There goes, Let's not f–k with mother nature."

On a night patrol along the coast searching for the Cong "bum boats" taking arms south about 0200, I told my team mate I was sleepy and he said he was wide awake. For some reason I peeked over at him a few minutes later and saw him nod. I played dead and watched. Soon his head dropped on his chest. I wrote a note to the crewmen that I was going to release a Parachute Flare to wake him up and not to be alarmed. I passed the note aft to the Radar Operator, armed the weapons panel and fired the flare. A loud Boom and a Bright flash of light!!! I thought my co-pilot was going through the over head hatch. He never nodded off again during our deployment.

On a night Catapult Launch I was flying right Seat and my Team Mate was in the left seat. We were taxing up to the Starboard Catapult and had stopped to await the plane ahead to be shot. I noticed the forms of two men out the window and flashlights flickering. The forms disappeared and we were launched. Upon return to the ship we discover that an Electronics Technician from the squadron had been told we had a radio problem. He was new to work the flight deck and almost walked into the propeller. Another experienced man saw him and grabbed him back. His right arm had flown out and his thumb was cut off by the prop. The flight deck is a dangerous place and these young men who work the deck deserve more pay than they are allowed. The spinning props are hard to see if the light is not shining on them from the right angle. The Navy has had men sucked up into the Jet Engine intakes, men killed by propellers, men blown over the side, men killed or maimed by a broken arresting cable flying past at over 100 miles per hour. The cold North Atlantic arctic winds and freezing rain do not stop flight deck activity. It is a very dangerous job.

On a day light coastal patrol we heard two Air Force pilots flying F4F Phantoms in our vicinity, say that the left engine was on fire. We were near Tiger Island and the wing man was telling the flight leader to get out of the airplane. Pilot and Radar Intercept Officer, (RIO), ejected and we saw the chutes coming down to the northeast of the island. I switched to Guard Channel and called for a Jolly Green (rescue helicopters) to rescue two men landing in the water. While awaiting their arrival, and as the pilots were drifting in their raft past the island we noticed splashes in the water and smoke coming from an island gun site. In just a few minutes two A4's an AD and another F4 arrived and started diving on the gun sites on the island. We had set up a race track pattern and dropped a smoke light so the Jolly Green could see the two men and the wind direction. We pulled further east so as not to get hit by the gun site and then have four more men in the water. The Jolly Green finally arrived and that pilot tried to set the Helo down into seven foot swells to pick up the pilots. The Helo rolled off the crest of the wave and the rotor blades started flying past our nose. Now there were six men in the water. We reported that fact while the four attack planes subdued the first and second gun sites on the island. Another rescue Helo arrived, picked everyone out of the water, and we all departed for home base.

Six months later my Team Mate and I received a Navy Commendation Medal for our part in the rescue. Many years after my retirement I was contacted by the

A4 Pilot attempting to arrange a reunion in New York aboard the carrier Intrepid. He informed me that we were mentioned in a book entitled "Fighting For Air" authored by TV Reporter "LIZ TROTTA" who is seen on Sunday Morning Fox news in the time frame 2009/2010. On page, 157 the rescued pilot states, "The next thing that happens I see an S2, an antisubmarine navy plane with a high wing and two piston engine. This stupid little airplane, and he's only doing about 150 knots and he's flying between me and the island, back and forth, and every time he goes by they stop shooting at me and start shooting at him. So I call the guy, 'Aircraft over tiger Island. Do you have me in sight?' 'Rog, I sure do.' It was a real calm and easygoing voice. I said, 'Man, they're shooting the shit out of you.' He says, 'Rog' and keeps flying back and forth drawing away the fire." The book may be obtained from the University of Missouri Press, Columbia and London.

During the Western Pacific Deployment the perks of being aboard an aircraft carrier permitted the entire crew to purchase goodies from the various ports visited. Several hundred motorcycles from Japan were stored on the hanger deck. The Commander Fleet Air Pacific had written a letter to discourage people from bringing home motorcycles due to several deaths contributed to those vehicles. My Commanding Officer had purchased a beautiful Kawasaki and had talked about how nice it would be to ride the bike from his residence on Coronado through the back gate to the squadron. He returned his bike to the dealer and wrote a sickening letter to the Admiral agreeing with the fact that motorcycles should not be brought home. I made a statement in the ward room at diner that the cows were going to be killed because a farmer had been kicked in the head while milking. Fortunately the Commanding Officer of the carrier did not fret about the Admirals letter. I bought the boys a nice Yamaha Trail Bike, and numerous other articles from Japan, Singapore, Hong Kong and the Philippines. Prior to our arrival at North Island the motorcycles were covered with brown paper and the Commander Fleet Air San Diego was led up the forward ladders to the Flag Bridge. The motorcycles were off loaded and taken off the base later that evening. Politically Correct crap!!!

I moved up to Commanding Officer of VS33. The squadron earned the Commander Naval Air Forces "E" for Excellence, the Captain Arnold Jay Isbell award for Anti-Submarine Excellence and The Flight Safety Award during the period that I was Commanding Officer. In October 1969 orders were received for Executive Officer of an Experimental Squadron in Key West, Florida. We had grown to three horses and had served a tour of duty in Key West with the Brazilians. None of the family wanted to return to Key West. I declined the orders and was told that I had seriously harmed my chances for promotion as the job was a "Shoe In" for Captain. I had achieved my goal as Commanding Officer and have never regretted the choice.

An opening as the Naval Aviation Representative with the Federal Aviation Administration Headquarters in Fort Worth, Texas was open for a Commander. I asked, and received orders to that duty. We moved to Ft Worth and rented a 10 acre mini farm with a four horse barn. I constructed a riding ring and Billie started teaching English Riding Lessons. She was in her realm. In just a few weeks she had students to keep her busy. Mike stayed in San Diego, Mark and Matt had a set of wheels, and

Mell was nine years of age. We enjoyed the farm life for two years and the boys had several nice long visits with Grandma prior to her passing.

The Navy, Air Force and Army representatives at the FAA Regional Headquarters are assigned to safe guard operating areas around the military bases and low level training routes. The Reps attend all meetings held regularly within the region from the southern border to the Canadian Border. I was an at home dad during this period, except for a few days on the road per month.

While mowing the ten acres shortly after moving in, Bubba, a 14 year old from up the road came over with the boys and had a bottle of Whiskey. He offered me a swig. I thought it was tea and took a good gulp. It was whiskey!!!!Welcome to the Ft Worth country!!!! The locals had made their own "Buckin' Bronco" by attaching a 55 gallon drum to inner tubes fastened to four trees. It was a favorite neighborhood game to ride the Bronco. Matt got "licks" at Keller School for opening all the unlocked locker doors on the way to the rest room and then running down the hall slamming them on the way back to class. A teacher had a hearing aid and she was taken in, one time only, by a student who mouthed his words. She turned up the volume and then he hollered out loud and blew her away. I never discover which boy did that!!!! Both were walking gingerly for a day or two!!! Three long hairs from Bonita Stable came to visit the summer we were to move back to California and the five of them terrorized the Sheriff's department for several weeks. "Git them long hairs out o' here!!!!" I discovered a six pack of beer hanging down in the cool water of the well, and cigarets in the barn. The five of them had fashioned an obstacle course for the Yamaha on the ten acres and had a great time with the motorcycle. None were injured fortunately!!!The family was comfortably seated around the living room watching TV one evening when we heard gravel being thrown on the porch. We all knew immediately that it was, BUBBA. I broke out the shot gun ran out and fired a round into the air. The next day Bubba came around scratching and itching his back side. He finally admitted that when he heard the blast he hit the ground and rolled onto a prickly thistle plant.

Billie and her students entered English Pleasure and Equitation Classes at the Ft. Worth Fat Stock Show in January, and also the Dallas Horse show in October. We met the "Horsy Crowd" including Ross Perot, who's daughter was showing Tennessee Walkers. She had a run of the mill horse. Billie suggested he visit a few of the well known stables and mount his daughter on a better horse. That he did and from that point on his daughter was earning Blue Ribbons. The daughter of the Chase Bank Empire told us that as a child they played with the Hope Diamond and would find it stuffed behind the cushions on the sofa. The family presented it to the Smithsonian. One of Billies teen age students won the Blue Ribbon over expensive Equitation Horses at the Dallas Show. Her horse had been purchased for $300 from a Plano Stable. Billie groomed the child and coached her from the rail. She won the class without a doubt. There were many upset parents that just knew their daughter would win. Where did this unknown child come from???? Billie could talk to horses and they would listen. I never, in all the years we had horses, could communicate with them as did Billie. Prior to leaving Ft Worth we bred Billie's mare with a beautiful stallion, Anacacho Shamrock stabled at Muenster, TX.

Bubba's family lived a short distance up the road and we became close friends and are still in touch with Betty and Junior, and their off spring. (2010). Junior retired from his construction trade and now has a nice place on Lake Whitney in Texas. I will never forget his description of his little dog. "That dog is plumb eat up with dumb." . While building the fence around the riding ring for Billie, I checked out a transit from the FAA and made the rails of the fence level. The ground sloped so the fence was high on one end and low on the other. Junior told me my fence was, "Plumb eat up with dumb!!!!" It did look stupid but I never got around to sawing the posts off at the same height. What the heck we're out in the country!!!! For those unfamiliar with Texas, Dallas is known as the Gate Way to the West and FT. Worth is known as the A-hole of the East. A joke among the Dallas-ites!!!

BACK TO SEA DUTY

On 4 August 1971 I detached from the FAA desk with orders to Report For Duty with Commander Cruiser/ Destroyer Flotilla THREE at Long Beach by 13 September as Intelligence Officer. The horses decided that San Diego would be our new home and we headed straight for that destination. Bradley's Stable, in Bonita, to unload the horses, Rustaway's Blu, The Light Fantastic, and Mr. Frank. I used my WWII GI Bill to purchase a new home on Golfcrest Dr. at the intersection of Mission Gouge Rd. Pending the closure on the house and the arrival of our furniture we spent a few weeks with a friend in the old neighborhood we had lived in earlier. We finally were able to move in and partially settle before I had to report to Long Beach. Our house was the last house on the street with a huge vacant field between the house and Mission Gorge. Matt took the Yamaha up on the lot and was riding around. A neighbor who lived across the street, name is forgotten, came over, pulled out an Honorary Sheriff's badge and told Matt to quit riding. Matt told the man to take his Kellogg Corn Flake badge and leave him alone, and to contact me if he had a complaint. The man never talked to me and I found out about the incident later. We will have future dealings with this neighbor. I reported for duty and for a month came home on weekends and on Wednesday nights. It was only 125 miles to Long Beach and the little Blue Opal ran like a top. I managed to hang the curtain rods prior to departing aboard the USS Chicago, a heavy Cruiser, for a seven month deployment to the Vietnam conflict. Being a member of the Admirals Staff was a whole different experience and we staffers were informed by the Chief of Staff that no one leaves the table until the Admiral pushes back his chair. I gained from 170 to 186 lbs even though my work space was three decks below the main deck and my other duties were eight decks above the main. Five to six trips per day up and down the ladders kept me in shape. Our Group became a member of the SEVENTH Fleet and we controlled all surface ships except the carriers. A funny incident that may be told was a briefing in which I relayed information that the Air Force had destroyed 24 trucks the previous day. The Admiral said, "Mo, do you know that the Air Force has destroyed more trucks than have ever been built in the entire world in this Vietnam conflict!!!!" During an in port trip to Subic Bay I took my last Navy flight in an S2 with an old squadron mate from VS 33. We flew around the islands and logged 2 hours.

The Chicago, and our staff received several awards for our services during that deployment, I was awarded the Bronze Star for my portion. We, departed the Chicago in the Philippines and flew into El Toro in a C141 Transport. Billie and the boys were there to greet me. She and the boys looked great!!!! Time for a coin toss in the grass!!!!!!! We arrived home and a phone call from the Chief of Staff advised not to unpack as the Group that had replaced us on the Cruiser Long Beach had all been killed in a Helicopter crash. We may have to go back!! An hour later the emergency had been resolved and I could expect further orders for a new assignment. Billie had taken control of the family in her usual proficient manner, Mell had been enrolled in Karate, Blu had been moved to another stable for training as a Hunter/Jumper and Mark was taking lessons to properly show the horse during the season. Both boys were working part time and when I arrived home every thing had been done about the house and yard except for a fence. Billie had several run ins with our nosy neighbor who had told the boys I had no business being in Viet Nam and leaving my family. We were in the driveway and he came over to start a fuss. Billie grabbed his necktie and pulled the knot into a small bead the size of a pea. I spun him in the direction of his house and gave him a swift kick in his rear. He filed a complaint with the city. We attended a meeting that resulted in his complaints being dropped and his Honorary Sheriff's Badge removed. It was during that meeting with a city lawyer that I lost faith in the judicial area. A statement was made that, "We take up law to make money. If I look out the window and see some one shoot a person and kill him, I will defend that person until he runs out of money." I told him he was immoral and left the office. The nosy neighbor turned to other pursuits and left our family alone. I suspect the neighborhood teenagers are the ones who blew his mail box to smithereens and egged his house repeatedly.

FINAL NAVY ORDERS

My orders were as Officer-in-Charge of Naval Air Maintenance Training Detachments West Coast with headquarters at Naval Air Station Memphis, Tennessee. We would not have to move and Billie could enjoy her horses and enter all the West Coast Horse Shows. My office was aboard the Naval Air Station North Island in San Diego. Detachments under my cognizance included Imperial Beach, North Island, Miramar, Pendleton, El Toro, Lemoore Moffet Field, Alameda and Whidbey Island. Each Detachment had it's own Commander. My responsibility was to provide the training necessary for the pilots, aircrewmen, and maintenance personnel to maintain the fleet at maximum efficiency. In my career I had attended school for over 26 years. The most efficient and knowledgeable instructors I ever encountered were the enlisted personnel who taught Navy classes. They didn't have Bachelor's or Master's or Piled Higher and Deeper Degrees, but they far out taught most of the college professors I had ever sat under. I maintained personal contact with each detachment and coordinated needs with the Commander Naval Air Forces Pacific Fleet..

The time frame for this three year period was May 1972 to June 1, 1975. It was family time and Billie and Mark were kept busy showing the Thorough-bred Hunter, Rustaway's Blu, and Billie's English Pleasure Horse, The

Light Fantastic. On June 23 1972, we were sitting in the den watching television and Billie suddenly said, "We need to go to the stable, I think Fan is ready to deliver!!!" Jumped into the car and arrived in time (1030 PM) to climb over the fence and help Fan drop her foal. It was an amazing bit of ESP that Billie had regarding her family.

Mell was into Karate and Matt was busy chasing skirts. Mark was in his 20's, Matt was17 and Mell was 12. Mike had taken advantage of his Photo lab experience in the Navy and was busy with NFL Football Games and International Soccer competitions. He was off every weekend in the US or Canada. In January 1974 I swore Mark into the Army and after recruit training in Missouri he elected to serve in Germany with a Helicopter Unit. His Eur-rail Pass allowed him to visit many cities and countries during his off time.

The colt had been put into Five Gaited Training and had progressed rather well. He was shown at the Del Mar Arena and won the Red Ribbon for his first class at two years of age. It was a beginning for his later years.

On a visit to Norman, Oklahoma to see Billie's father we learned of a ten acre spot with a small house that was for sale at only $23,000. Since I was planning on retiring at the end of this assignment it was not economically feasible to remain in San Diego and pay the board and feed for four horses. Billie's horses were like dogs and cats. You just don't dispose of the pets. We purchased the 10 acres and turned it over to a Real Estate to rent until time to retire. We received the first and last months rent and that was it. The "Wealthy" Texan with the expensive western suit and Stetson Hat was a cheat. He was on Social Security Disability. We found out after he had trashed the place, that he worked on the sly with the

Chevy Dealer in town, and that he was not so disabled that he could break raw horses and sell them at a higher price. The neighbor told us she watched him ride the bucking horses and was not disabled in any way. I paid an attorney to force him out of the house. No one knew where he moved and I was informed that even a judge would not be told where his Social Security checks were being mailed. If I could find him and pay for the police to go and bring him to Norman for prosecution I may be able to be paid for the rent and damage to the house. It was useless to proceed.

My retirement was set for 31 May 1975 and closed 27 ½ years of Naval Service. Housing prices were climbing steadily and we had no trouble selling the house for a profit. Mike was settled in San Diego, Matt was tied up with his girl friend, Mark was in Germany so Mom, Mo and Mell with a new puppy, named Flipper departed for Norman, Ok. The horses would be picked up at the stable and would follow within a few weeks. Our little house on 10 acres was a mess. We tore out the carpets, scrubbed it down, repainted the rooms and moved in. We hired a bull dozer operator to level an area for a riding ring, horse barn and outside corrals and to bury an old car and lots of trash. The University of Oklahoma was in the process of demolishing the WWII barracks and buildings and I purchased all the lumber I would need to build the barn, riding ring and fences at half the price from a lumber yard. My first goal was to build corrals for the arrival of the horses. This was accomplished in high humidity and heat. I had a bucket of cold water from the well and a large towel dripping around my head and neck while I hammered the boards to the posts. I estimated completion of the corrals within two weeks and we sent for the horses to be delivered to a stable in Edmond, a suburb of Oklahoma City. The driver had other stops and finally off loaded our four horses after three days on the road. We had been told the driver would come straight through from San Diego to Oklahoma City. It was reported to us that upon their arrival Mr. Frank and the other horses were standing in manure up their hocks. They had obviously never been let out to walk around during the entire trip. Mr. Frank died in a few days. The driver was eventually fired.

The corrals were completed, the horses were delivered, construction of the barn was commenced and we had purchased four calves for $25 each that we fed and housed at night in a ramshackle shed on the property. We fed the calves by bottle while standing astride their bodies while they drained the milk. It was real fun for Billie and I but Mell was not too interested and had found a friend up the road to play with. I did manage to have him hold on to a gasoline driven hole driller for about one hour one afternoon. We finally gave up and dug the holes by hand as the gas driven bit would dig into the earth and pull down while we were fighting to pull it up. Enough of that torture!!!

A huge thunderstorm came up during an afternoon and from the kitchen window we could see the lightning strike a posts near Blu's head. He jumped about six feet sideways. The burners on the electric stove were covered in a purplish haze and we lost the phone line. That settled it, a storm cellar was needed. We hired that construction and stored our keep sakes such as photo albums and papers down in the cellar. Mistake, they all molded around the edges after a time. A heat lamp and moisture absorption material was the solution. During the three years on the farm we used that cellar many times as Oklahoma is in the Tornado Belt

Billie's father, Eurial Vivian George, a retired State Representative, State Senator and rancher had remarried and was living in Norman after the death of his wife. He, at one time, had 480 head of White Faced Herefords on some 1500 acres of leased land from the Indian owners. He bragged that he had a name for each of them. I could not get him to come out to the farm to see our horses and calves. It said it made him homesick. We settled instead for some delicious apple and pecan pie his wife served us during our visits. He passed away at the age of 87 while we were living in Oklahoma.

July through September passed rapidly for us as the barn building project took all of our labor. It was a Pole barn measuring 24 by 72 feet that would contain four horse stalls, a tack room, a feed room and wash rack at the end. The pillars were 14 foot poles sunk into concrete filled holes and then framed to be covered in corrugated galvanized iron siding and roofing. The only help I purchased were the roof trusses to cover the 24 foot span. Mell helped me slide the trusses onto the supporting rafters. He and his friend were busy hunting and playing guitar. He attended the Noble School and was earning great grades. Matt had moved he and his girl friend to Norman and lived in town. No help there. I finished the barn, mounted an electrical box to the side and called for the City Inspector. Received an "A" for barn wiring and we were in business with a green tag so that the electric company could run the wires to the barn. A slight breather and then on to the Riding Ring.

I was busy digging post holes for the ring and one of the orange electrical trucks pulled into the field. They said, "Move over, we have been watching you bust your butt on this place and we are going to drill the post holes for you in this sand stone." They stopped by on their lunch break for several days and drilled all the holes. I got them to accept two bottles of Whiskey for their help. They were just good Okies out to help a neighbor. I would nail the boards and Billie followed with the White Paint. We finished the ring and then covered the front with a nice white fence and swinging gate. A carved sign naming our ten acres as Shamrock Valley Farm. The hard work was over and we spent two and a half years enjoying the peace and serenity.

Our first years garden measured 60 by 30 feet. We planted a flat of some 60 tomato plants and Billie canned seventy quarts of tomatoes and 105 quarts of tomato juice. We had potatoes under the house keeping them cool, egg plant by the dozen, peas, carrots, turnips and hours of labor trying to keep ahead of the ripening plants. Big Mistake!!!! Our second garden was a 10 by 10 footer and even that was too much for the three of us. I experimented with selling Life Insurance Policies to university seniors. I was spending more money on gasoline than I was making and gave that up as a bad choice. Billie had several riding students and we attended all the horse shows from Dallas to Kansas City during the season. Norman was Billie's place of birth and she lived there until age 14 when she joined her mother in Corpus Christi. One of her distant cousins was Tommy Sturdevant who was a Major League Pitcher for the Yankees in 1956. We had met him at that time in Oklahoma City and he mentioned he was going to put the bite on Casey Stengel for $65,000 for the 1957 season. Now ball players are in the millions!!!! Tommy was a jovial story teller and would have the entire gathering in stitches telling stories about the Yankees and Casey at our get togethers on the farm.

Billie and I attended one Oklahoma University football game. We were seated behind three broad shouldered men who jumped up at the slightest activity and completely blocked our view. Another half drunk man was seated about eleven seats in from the aisle and every time the hot dog or pop corn vender passed he would order something that had to be passed down the row. The lady seated next to me said, "The next thing he orders lets all just squeeze it." It was a hot dog. He received a wrapper full of mush!!!! From then on we stayed at home and watched football on the TV!!!!We repaired the ramshackle shed and bought some baby chicks at the feed store. Half turned out to be fryers which we devoured. The remainder were yielding small white eggs with pale yellow yolks. Billies uncle told us to throw a flake of alfalfa into the shed and in just a few days we had turned the yolks to orange and the best tasting eggs I have ever eaten. It turned out that one of our four calves was a bull. He did his duty and our herd jumped to six head, one baby died at birth. They roamed the back seven acres and kept the field neatly mowed.

Flipper our Australian Sheep dog puppy had grown and one morning he was barking at the kitchen window. Way out in the back of the property we could see movement. We finished breakfast and walked out to see what it was. There was a herd of 22 goats that had gotten through the fence. Without any movement on our part, Flipper slowly moved back and forth in front of the herd, turned them and herded them back through the fence. It was an amazing display of instinctive herding that is attributed to the Australian Sheep Dogs. Flipper could load a horse into the trailer without any barking, or guidance from

Billie or I, and then look at us for thanks. That breed of dog is the reason you find them around many horse stables. They are a mixture of the Queensland Heeler and Dingo from Australia.

By the third year Billies father had passed, her childhood close friend was dying of cancer, Tommy's parents had passed, we seldom had visitors unless we provided the steaks and drinks and we were working dawn to dusk mowing and keeping up with all the animals. We decided to move back to San Diego and rejoin our old friends. Mell had graduated from Norman High, Mark had returned from his three year stint in Europe, Matt and his girl friend were settled in Norman. The property sold in a matter of weeks and the sale included the chickens, cows, goat, rabbits and an older stray dog. Address is 2919 SE 89th St., Norman, Oklahoma. We pulled out hauling a 25 foot Coachman Bunk house Travel Trailer. The horses were to be delivered to Bradley's Stable in Bonita . The house we had purchased in 1964 for $17,100 was now in the $60,000 bracket. The home on Golfcrest we had paid $38,500 was over $100,000. Housing had escalated out of sight. We purchased a Mobile Home in Spring Valley in the Lamplighter Village Park for cash. It measured 70 by 24 feet and was very roomy and comfortable and had a storage lot for the travel trailer. Mark moved out on his own and Mell joined with some friends and rented their own apartment. Mom and Mo finally had their own nest!!!!!I took employment with an Elevator Manufacturing Company and several months later went to work for General Dynamics Electronics Division at the Lindbergh Field Plant. Our week ends again were with the "Horsy Set". We had many friends in San Diego and there was always a party to go to.

Bradley's stable was hit with a major catastrophe on a Monday morning. Nineteen horses were found dead in their stalls and our Hunter, Blu was seriously ill. Billie stayed with the horse for almost a week with just a few breaks to clean up and rest. Veterinarians from all over the state combed the stables for some sign of poisonous weeds that may have caused the deaths. To qualify as a farm for tax purposes the stable always had a few head of cattle and some chickens running around. The feed for the cattle and the feed for the horses were stored in same shed. New hands unfamiliar with the feed, mixed the cattle feed with the horse feed. The cattle feed contained a substance named Rumincin which is used to fatten cattle. It was discover by a veterinarian in Ames Iowa who was doing autopsies on the dead horses. Good for cattle but deadly for horses!!!! Blu was a valuable horse at this time and had taken the Yellow Ribbon (3rd Place) at a Major Horse Show in which 162 horses had been entered in the class. The Judge split the class into four sections and then selected six horses from each group. Blu won third place out of the final 24 horses. We had no intention of suing the stable for the loss. However a few days before the time limit for legal action expired a news article mentioned that the Stable had filed suit against the feed company for damages. We then filed suit against the Stable and received a settlement that partially offset the loss of a wonderful horse.

I had established contact with my mother and sister and was notified that mother had suffered a stroke and was in very poor health. To be closer to Columbus, Ohio I transferred to the Boeing Airplane Company in Wichita, Kansas. We rented the Mobile home and moved to Kansas taking only the partially trained colt.

On a visit to Columbus, Billie was feeding my mother some Chicken Noodle Soup when mother said, "Billie, I guess I had you pegged wrong all these years, I am sorry." She had missed out on her grand children by being so stubborn and close minded all those years. I carried her to the car and we took a memory lane ride through her childhood neighborhood. That area has been restored and is on the south side of Columbus, called German Town. Mother told me she got a good spanking for riding on the back of a boys motor cycle as a young teen aged girl. She had been a Milliner as a young lady and had been sent to New York City to model ladies hats prior to her marriage. She once again had a nice ride to visit all her youthful days. I was surprised that the small house she was born in had been occupied by the family of nine persons. We said our final good byes!!!! Her wish, like my father's was to be cremated.

We departed Columbus,(April 1981) heading south, to visit Mike and Tanya's new son in Camden, Arkansas. I was notified that mother had passed away and that Christina, (my sister), had every thing under control. Our first Grandson, Shawn Michael Schaer, was born November 1980. He was just a few months old and we spent several days sight seeing and enjoying our visit. Billie was enthralled with the baby and said it was like having Mike all over again. She carried him around for three days!!!Mike and Tanya were enlarging the house and had opened a Photo Shop in Camden. However as with all small towns a newcomer is not often welcomed with open arms. Mike had taken many photos of a local town event and had posted the photos on his shop bulletin board with tear off order blanks. Instead of ordering the numbered photos the people just took the pictures. They tried very hard to make a go of it, in Camden but soon closed shop and returned to La Jolla, CA.

Billie and I had a slow leisurely trip returning to Wichita and stopped on the way home to visit an old Navy buddy, Joe Gass and his wife who had settled on 30 acres near Lake of the Ozarks. Joe and his wife had attended one of numerous Navy parties dressed in two cardboard boxes painted like gas pumps. She was Ethyl and He was High Test. It was nice to just be alone without changing diapers or feeding and caring for young ones. Billie and I throughly enjoyed our companionship and marriage and stopped at every roadside attraction and motel like newly weds. No jelly beans were required any longer. We visited Billie's relatives, Betty and Arnold and their daughter, Rajean and the twins, in Estes Park, CO; Yoder Kansas, an Amish Community with horse and wagon, Kansas City and the Truman Home, a town settled by Swede's with all their pastries and baked goods.

During our stay in Kansas Billie showed the colt at numerous horse shows. He was awarded Reserve Champion Five Gated at the end of the year 1980 for the State of Kansas. I was on a one year contract with Boeing and continued working after the contract to finish several projects for the electronic assemblies we were manufacturing. The Masonic order is very heavy in Wichita and they have fantastic parades to promote their various charities and especially the Children's Burn Hospital. My working partner was a Mason and told me the only thing secret about the order is that a person has to ask to become a member. The members are not permitted to solicit membership. However it is a close knit organization and the supervisors and managers at Boeing were all masons. I was told it was impossible to promote to a manager level if you were not a mason. Another interesting tid-bit was a man seated in our area who had recently resigned his position with the government as a Social Security Fraud Investigator. He said that in two years work he never got a fraud case before a Judge because the witnesses had been threatened by the accused that their house would be burned to the ground if they testified against him. As a result no witness would show for the trial and the Judge threw out the case.

We returned to San Diego in late 1981 and were able to move back into the Mobile Home after a short time of living in the travel trailer. I was offered the same job I had left with a nice salary increase to match the Boeing pay. The couple who had leased Billie's English Pleasure Horse said the mare had gotten into the feed room and foundered on a torn bag of sweet feed. She was lame in both front hoofs. We took the horse back. Bradley's Stable in Bonita had been forced to move because the City of Chula Vista had voted to make the Bonita Valley a Green belt area without stables. We boarded the Mare and her offspring at a new location named Willow Glen in the El Cajon area. It wasn't long before Billie had organized a Mounted Troop consisting of 20 horses. My horse's name was "Uwee" because he sometimes, without warning, would do a quick 180 degree U Turn and the unsuspecting rider would go off on the ground. One of our riders was rather severely handicapped with dyslexia and we had to position her so that the rider ahead of her could always point the direction in which she should turn during our maneuvers. Between "Uwee" and Miss Dyslexia we had some laughable happenings during our horse show intermissions with the Willow Glen Mounted Riding Troop. (F-Troop for short).

Bradley had relocated his Bonita stable in an area east of El Cajon called Dehesa. We moved our two horses into Dehesa as soon as the horse barn was constructed. We Tried every known remedy to treat the foundered mare with no success. She was in constant pain and could barely walk on her sore front hooves. Our veterinarian euthanized the horse and she was buried on the grounds at Dehesa. Mr. Bradley had picked up a nice horse at an auction that had been originally purchased for $50,000 for a young teen aged girl living in Rancho Santa Fe. Upon her graduation from High School, it was off to college, and the horse was put up for sale. A lameness in a front leg discouraged many potential buyers and Mr. Bradley obtained the horse. Billie and I bought the Gelding for $1500. The name was Red Marble and he was a natural Three Gaited English Show Horse. He was head strong and the inside of his mouth was callused from a bicycle chain bit that some trainer had fashioned to attempt better control. Billie backed him off the harsh bits and in her instinctive way obtained the horse's trust. A Silvergate Riding Club of which we had been members had fallen into a dormant state. Billie and I revived the club by putting on two yearly consecutive horse shows with very little assistance from the former members. Billie personally obtained financial sponsors for every class, I typed the program, and had them printed, and after work, for several hours each night, constructed new jumps and obstacles for the Hunter classes. Red Marble had been shown and his name was well known in the horse circuit. In the fall show of 1985 Billie was awarded the Silvergate Riding Club Challenge Trophy above 14 other exceptional Saddlebred Horses. A Blue Ribbon Ride all the way, even the losers cheered as the contestants had all followed the show career of Red Marble.

During this period of working and horse shows our children had been busy. Matt had married Debra in 1983 in Norman, Oklahoma and we towed the Travel Trailer to the wedding. Betty and Junior our Ft. Worth neighbors joined us at the camp ground. It was a beautiful ceremony and all parents of both sides had an enjoyable get together. Junior commented that the wedding was "Plumb eat up with nice." Meanwhile Mell and his wife, Teresa, presented us with our second grand child, Marcus William in 1985. They resided in El Cajon and we were constantly in touch.

I was temporarily working on a dual proposal with Grumman Aircraft on Long Island, in 1986, when Billie called to tell me that upon my return home we were going to learn to CLOG Dance. We had been Line Dancing at the Mobile Home Park and had learned all the instructors dances. To further our experience we had been branching out to some of the bars in the area to learn new dances. Billie had gone with the other ladies to the Circle "D" in El Cajon, CA while I was on assignment. At an intermission, the record Rocky Top Tennessee was played and a troupe of people jumped onto the floor and started clogging. This was a whole new experience and proved to be addictive as every time you think there is no other way to move your feet you are shown new steps. Clogging is fast and fun, a few couples dances, but primarily group performances. It had moved across the country from the east coast and many clubs had started in California. We were hooked and never missed a session. I would slip out to the stable to feed the horses and then return to dancing. The stable manager called on a Sunday evening after I had fed to tell us that Red Marble was down. We found the horse lying in the stall, contacted our vet and Billie started walking the horse. I checked the feed and found teeny little black ants all over the sweet feed. The vet said that had nothing to do with the illness. He determined that the horse must have rolled in the stall and twisted a gut. The next day he withdrew fluid from his belly and it was bloody. He told Billie the horse would not last 48 hours. I believe that Billie walked that horse the entire time. She was determined to keep Red alive but it was no use. We were down to one stallion.

Clogging became our past time and we never missed a session. A close friend and co-worker age 57 was playing with his children shooting baskets in their drive way and keeled over with a massive heart attack. I made the decision at that time to stop working at age 62. Matt and Debbie informed us that the oil bust of 1987 had hit Oklahoma hard and houses were for sale at very reasonable prices. We took a trip to Norman and located a nice brick home with a large yard including a pool for only $79,000. We moved the furniture into the house in December of 87 and were welcomed with a severe Ice Storm that stranded everyone for two days. There were diamonds glistening on every tree and it was a beautiful sight to behold. In February 1988 I retired from General Dynamics and we, Mom, Mo the colt and one dog, Flipper moved to Norman, Oklahoma at 3118 Walnut Rd. In April 1988 Mell informed us that James Michael Schaer had arrived. Our third grand child. We would be taking the Motor Home back to San Diego for Christmas!!!!

As a child growing up in Norman, Billie had taken dancing lessons in a small studio near the University Campus Corner. She also sang on the Sunday Morning

Cain's Coffee Hour with station WKY in Oklahoma City with Smiley Burnett (Frog). Unknown to her father, Billie and her mother went to the studio on the pretense of going to church. One Sunday morning her father happened to be listening to the radio and heard them announce little Billie Jeanne is going to sing and dance to the song, "Dance with the Dolly with the Hole in her Stockin." He was furious and upon their return to the house they were told, "No daughter of mine is going to Hollywood and become a 'Chippy!!! You will not be singing on the radio any more!!!" Billie was very talented and several times mentioned that her father had deprived her of a singing, dancing and acting career.

After settling into the new house Billie decided to teach clog dancing in late 1988. We tiled the garage, purchased four large mirrors from a defunct business, purchased the sound equipment and put an ad in the newspaper. It took but a few weeks to over flow our small space. Parking became a problem and we moved to the Norman Recreation center to avoid problems in the neighborhood. We were soon busy four evenings a week with beginner, intermediate and advanced classes for children and adults. My task was to set up and take down the equipment, I was the gofer this and that!!! I soon eased the load on Billie by taking over the beginner classes. This involved eight dances with a few new steps in each and a desire to learn more. It seemed each week there were new people eager to join in the fun and exercise of Clogging. As we learned of other groups throughout Oklahoma we organized the Oklahoma Clogging Association. The state measures 331 miles east and west and 235 miles north and south, not counting the Pan Handle section. Our meetings were to be held every two months. After several long drives from the outer fringes to the center the meetings dwindled to non attendance. The club was dissolved after two years and all agreed to donate the $1200 in the Treasury to the Saint Jude's Children's Cancer Hospital in Memphis. The hospital suggested that Video Games and toys were sorely needed. Billie and I purchased two 39 gallon trash bags full of games and toys for the kids and dropped them off on the way to a National Clogging Convention in Nashville. We were told a Plaque would be positioned at the Entrance showing the donation from the Oklahoma Clogging Association.

Mell and Terry delivered Lauren Teresa in January of 1990 and Matt and Debbie delivered Simone Alexandra in June of 1990, our fourth and fifth grand children. Later on Mell's family grew to four children with the birth of Stephen Timothy in February 1992 and Matt and Debbie welcomed Sydney Allison in August of 1992, our sixth and seventh grand children. The year 1994 brought Slater Alexander in February, our eighth and final grand child. Our first Great Grand Child Jax Hurley was recently born in February 2010 to Shawn and Morgan in Fayetteville, AR.

These family additions were interspersed with travels across the nation to participate in fun filled clogging workshops and assemblies. The largest of all was the National gathering, usually around Thanksgiving Holiday. This group of over 6000 attendees pulled in cloggers from Australia, Germany, Czechoslovakia, Canada, Japan and every state in the USA. The favored spot was Opryland Hotel in Nashville where we had 6240 cloggers all dancing to the tune of Rocky Top Tennessee at the same time. Guinness Book of Records photographed the occasion but said that we had been beaten out by 6400 tap dancers in New York City. Other National Assemblies were San Diego, Memphis, Dallas and Orlando.

Shortly after moving to Norman in 1989 I received word that my sister, Christina, in Columbus had fallen and broken her upper arm and was being taken to the cleaners with a lady she had allowed to move into the house. My cousin Betty had visited and said the entire downstairs was stuffed with bags of items purchased at the flea market. There was barely enough room to wade through the foyer and living room. Every chair, sofa and table was covered in brown paper bags stuffed with dolls and clothing and items purchased by this woman. I drove to Columbus and found Christina in a dazed condition. The Emergency Room doctor admitted her to the hospital as her electrolytes were out of kilter, she had evidently taken too many Lasix pills. I discovered that this woman had talked her into listing her as a Pay on Death for several Certificates of Deposit and had her bank account and the House changed to will those assets to her. When Christina regained her senses I was appointed Power of Attorney and eliminated the Bag Lady and moved her out. Matt had taken the trip with me and between the two of us we got to the bottom of the conspiracy which had occurred between the Bag Lady and another Black woman living up the street. The medicine over dose had been engineered by the black lady. Apparently the Bag Lady would ask for twenty dollars every morning to go to the Flea Market and Christina, who was very gullible would give it to her. This woman had gone through $50,000 of Christina's and our mothers savings in over a four year period. The neighbor across the street told me that she would leave the house and walk around the corner out of sight and take a taxi to the Flea market. Another man was walking Chris's dog for about five minutes three times a week and she was paying him $20 for each walk. I returned with the motor home, cleaned out the house and put it up for sale. Chris and I spent a nice leisurely drive from Columbus to Oklahoma in the Motor Home and she was safely housed in a nice retirement center close to our house. In 1993 she suffered a Brain Stem Stroke and passed away peacefully in the early morning hours at age 71.

Christina was four years older than me. Aunt Norma told me she had been born on the kitchen table and the cord was wrapped around her neck. Called a "Blue Baby". Whether or not that affected her brain is not known. However she was a girl who would have been in her clime to have lived out in the country feeding the chickens and doing the chores. I remember my mother fixing her hair for school all during our young years. Chris never wore lip stick or rouge and was not interested in boys. She had one date with a young man and when they arrived home after a movie he tried to kiss her. She said she didn't want anyone slobbering over her face. No more dates for Chris. After graduating from East High School in June of 1939 she was employed at the Timken Roller Bearing Plant on Cleveland Ave. in Columbus as a bearing inspector. The girls on the line would rotate each of the roller bearings under a lamp to detect any cracks or flaws. It was piece work and there was a quota that had to be met each day. A very monotonous job but it was right up her alley. Several times she was offered a promotion to line boss but refused and stated she liked what she was doing and did not want to change. For 39 years she was a steady employee and as far as I know she never missed work. She awakened at 0530, caught the street car at 0600 and was at work at 0630 until 3 PM every day the plant was open. When I was discharged from the Navy in 1946, Christina had a Green Cushman Motor Scooter that she rode out into the country for enjoyment. She knew every farmer withing 15 miles of our home. She would just stop in, ask if she could feed the chickens or help out and swap canned goods that Mom had made for some the farmers wife had. In the winter when it got cold she would wear long underwear that was visibly white on her legs. If kids would look funny at her legs she would give them a few words about being polite and say, "Haven't you ever seen long underwear, smell the coffee!!!" The girls on the line at Timkens would tease each other by rubbing Limburger Cheese on their lamps and other tricks unknown to me. Chris saved every penny and then allowed the Bag Lady to move in and spend half of her savings. Had my cousin not called me all of her savings and the house would have gone to that slob. On our earlier visits to Columbus she and Matt got along famously and they rode the street car and later the trolley bus down town for a shopping trip. Mark was not so well liked as we had taken a hike out to Alum Creek and while walking along the path Mark mumbled, "Chris is sooo fat." She heard it and gave him a piece of her mind about being rude. When Dad first bought the 1932 used car he tried to teach her to drive at Franklin Park. If she turned the wrong way he would cuss and holler and she just gave up. Mom was the same way. If some one else had given them driving lessons they could have enjoyed an automobile all their lives. Instead they were dependent upon the street cars and trolley buses to go to the stores and shopping.

While I am on street cars, a favorite trick at Halloween was for one of us kids to stand in the car stop and when the street car stopped and opened the door the other kid would pull down the trolley and both would run off into the darkness. The conductor would have to get out and walk back to reinstall the trolley to the wires. We were little devils. Every once in a while an older brother would give us .22 gauge blank cartridges that we would place on the rail. When the street car ran over them they would sound like a machine gun. Famous criminals of that era were John Dillinger and Pretty Boy Floyd.

During the 1990's our group "The Sooner Clogging Company" participated in all the parades in Norman and Oklahoma City, the Oklahoma State Fair, Rest Homes, Schools, Churches, Octoberfest, and other organized gatherings. The mothers and adults would make costumes and everyone pitched in to the fun of dancing for the enjoyment of the spectators. The parents were delighted that their children seemed to grow up in front of their eyes and gain an aura of composure from performing for others. We had the young children's group from 7 to 10 years, teenagers, young adults, and grown ups. At one time we were 75 dancers strong and the men had to rush up to keep the huge speakers from rocking off the stage at the Electric CO-OP gatheringof over 4500 persons. Billie was always giving of herself for the kids and she spent more than she made by treating the group to Pizza after their lessons and for lunch after the long parades.

In the late 1990's when Michael Flatley introduced his Feet of Flames Irish Dancers, Billie remarked that she knew a lot of those steps and had been taught at nine years of age in Norman dance classes. "I am going to start teaching Irish Dancing also!!!" Bingo!! In two weeks she had a class full of youngsters eager to dance like Michael Flatley's dancers. Soon she had children and adults, the parents were eager to sew green vests and skirts to match for all the students. The first performance was in the Oklahoma City St. Patrick's Day Parade and they won a trophy for their exuberant performance.

A special treat for the cloggers was to participate in the annual Cloggers Showcase held the second weekend in May on the Riverwalk, Arneson Stage, on Friday and Saturday evenings. The Sooner Cloggers were invited to join with all the Texas Clogging Groups and to my knowledge they are still performing annually and are expected again this May of 2010.

Throughout the time frame 1988 to 1999 we were not only actively dancing four evenings per week and performing on many weekends, but at home I had built three large wooden decks. Two around the pool and a large 20 x 24 foot fenced deck off the master bedroom. The back yard was barren when we bought the home and Billie had turned it into a beautiful flowered and treed garden of Eden. Matt's family was growing up and Mell would visit from California in the summer. The pool was "L" shaped with a diving board and slide and our back yard entertained the family and the cloggers with many swim parties over the years. All the trees and shrubs required daily cleaning of the pool from tree leaves and bugs of the night. We were very active. I had installed a six foot wrought iron fence around the front yard with a large gate that was manually opened and closed. In about June of 2000 we returned home from shopping and one of our house dogs ran out into the street and was hit by a pick up. The dog was yelping and flopping around and Billie reached out for the collar and was bitten on the finger. We cleaned the bite and thought nothing of it. A week later it became infected and was Xrayed and the diagnosis was possibly arthritis or calcium deposit or it could be Osteomyelitis. The doctor was concerned and prescribed heavy antibiotics. Billie was slowing down and I noticed that she was no longer up in front of her classes but would sit by the equipment and have the younger girls show new steps.

EUROPE TRIP

We decided to obtain passports and to give up the dancing and take advantage of our military flight privileges. We closed shop and in October enjoyed a wonderful drive to Dover Delaware Air Force Base where we were scheduled for a flight to Ramstein, Germany. Dover is a beautiful City and the first State of the United States was full of historical sights while awaiting our departure. A huge tree in the town square area measured over six feet across. Billies outstretched arms did not cover the width of the trunk. Our flight to Europe was aboard an Air Force C5 transport plane. There were 32 steps up a truck mounted stair case into the passenger compartment just forward of the vertical tail. The flight was only partially filled and we were told October is a good month to fly because the children are back in school and most military families are settled for the year. Seven hours later after a great circle route we landed at Ramstein Air Force Base in Germany and obtained quarters for the night on the base. A car rental unit was located next to the quarters and we settled in for a short nap prior to a drive into the village of Kaiserslautern. Narrow streets and side by side row houses with everything neat as a pin. The church with a clock was the center piece of the town. Everyone was speaking English so there was no language problem. We soon discovered that using the credit card avoided a lot of trouble with money exchanging and trying to figure out what things were costing. After visiting the Base Exchange and sending a few cards to the kids we started out on the road into Switzerland to my fathers birthplace called Dagmersellen. Towns visited on the route were Saarbrucken, Strasbourg, then into Switzerland at Basel, Zurich and my father home towns at Willisau and Dagmersellen I had been using the internet to contact the Zurich news paper and sent the editor photos of my fathers relatives standing on a street corner. I asked him to publish the photos to try and establish contact with relatives. When we arrived the editor told me he had forgotten all about it and the photos were still in his "IN" basket. "Thanks a lot for nothing!!" We made inquiries at the local bed and bar but no one could shed light on my father's family. The police station was only open on Wednesday and the Church was locked up with a chain and padlock. I knew then why my father had left home at 18 years of age. Dagmersellen was a nice neat little village on the side of a hill with a few apple trees and a couple of cows munching grass. Nothing there to hold a young man to that area. Our bed was a mattress with a dull pink mattress cover and no sheets. My wife asked for some bed sheets. The proprietor said, "Sheets!!! Vas ist sheets!!!!" She pulled a gray dirty looking comforter out of the closet and indicated that you sleep on the mattress and cover with the scruffy looking comforter. We were refunded our cash and went into a regular hotel for the night. We had sheets but no wash cloths. The reason being that the customers steal them. You just wet the end of the towel for the wash rag. The little town of Willisau was full of shops. It seems that the locals close up for several hours for lunch and a nap and then reopen in the late afternoon and stay open until evening. The country side was green and beautiful. Everything was spotlessly clean. I spoke with numerous elderly villagers about my father and showed his birth certificate with his parents names but no one could give me any information.

We had heard that travel on the Autobahn was unlimited speed. However at 60 miles per hour we were part of the traffic and were never passed by speeding vehicles. I wondered if the 120 kilometer reading of the speedometer had been mis-interpreted to mean miles per hour. Throughout our entire road trip we never were passed by zooming vehicles.

From our fruitless search for my fathers background we continued to the cities of Bern, Lausanne and Geneva. Since Billie was not up to much walking most of our sight seeing was done from driving around the cities and just looking. There are no Motels along the highways to stop and spend the night. We were forced to rest in expensive Hotels that ran up to $200 per night. Again with no wash cloths. The hotel in Geneva boasted the worlds tallest clock. The dial was on the ninth floor and the pendulum extended downward to the main floor. From our breakfast table we could see the snow capped peaks and off into the distance about 60 miles one could see the peak of the famous Matterhorn Mountain.

From Geneva we crossed into France and headed for Paris. To this point we had been able to converse in English. However the French seem to delight in not speaking English even though our young troops are buried on their soil so that they are not speaking German. There was a noticeable difference in the attitude of the French, a resentment of Americans. We arrived in Paris and our first stop was to be the Eiffel Tower. We had seen the tower from several miles south of the city. As we entered into the traffic trying to find out which direction to go to the tower several shrugs of the shoulder were the answer to our query. Our first stop was to inquire for a room at the French Officers Quarters. They were booked for the night but reserved a room for the next night. We located a quaint Hotel, The Belfast, close by the Arc De Triomphe and parked the car in an underground parking lot. After breakfast we set out to see the sights. Walking was out of the question so we retrieved the car and entered into the Paris traffic. A six lane circle around the Arc with horns tooting and 2 inch spacing between fenders and we escaped and made our way to the Eiffel Tower. Billie grimaced but said, " I am going to get out and walk around this place." She and I spent the morning at the tower examining all the details and taking videos. Photos do not capture the enormity of the footings for this structure. We went from there to a river boat ride down the Seine. Statues of golden painted horses, golden domes on the buildings and beautiful architecture abounded on both sides. We glided past Notre Dame, the Louvre, the National Assemble, under beautiful bridges adorned with statues of heros of the past. We continued sight seeing from the car into the evening when we returned to the tower which is illuminated with orange lighting and is a spectacle to behold. Dinner at the Officer's Club and we retired with the knowledge that it would take at least a month to see the wonders of Paris, France. Since our rental car was not to leave the continent we were on our way back to Ramstein via Luxembourg. It was then that we remembered that we had forgotten the Can Can Dancers at the Paris Moulin Rouge. That had been on our agenda for Paris!!!

Reims, France was the next city on our route and we stopped in the town square which was a cobble stoned area at least 300 feet across and several block in length surrounded on all sides with shops. A nice river running through the town was being used by several rowing teams out for their practice session. The coaches rode along the river bank on a bicycle and hollered instruction to the rowers. All of these villages and cities were neat and clean, no trash could be seen any where. We stopped at a World War I cemetery of German Soldiers killed during the war. All the crosses were black. Later we stopped at a World War I cemetery of Americans killed in the war and all the crosses were white. I do not know the reason for the different color. We caught sight of a young lady exercising her Hunter/Jumper horse in their riding ring. Billie had to watch her practice and we spent an hour visiting and chatting about horses and showing. We arrived in Luxembourg in the evening. The Belair Hotel had a garage door next to the entrance. We were told to drive the car to the door, honk the horn and enter an elevator to the garage level. A nice secure spot for the car. Breakfast was a feast of breads, meats, pan cakes and eggs to satisfy any ones fancy. Luxembourg is a privately owned country and is completely controlled by The Grand Duke. Everyone pays their taxes to that family. It was a Sunday and we drove around the town for about two hours and proceeded on through Saarbrucken and to Ramstein to sign up for a flight to England for the next afternoon.

The Officer's Quarters were completely filled due to an annual training exercise. We were told by the car rental clerk of a quaint bed and breakfast house in town and that we could probably get a room for the night.

She also told us that we could just leave the car, with the keys, in their parking spot at the base when we left on our flight. After obtaining a room for the night we drove into Kaiserslautern for more sight seeing and also the little town of Landstuhl just outside the base where there is located a large Military Hospital that has been prominent in the news all during the Iraq war of the 2000's. We had time to package and mail a box of trinkets purchased for the kids prior to boarding our flight to Mildenhall Air Base in England. We spent the night on the base and in the morning proceeded to the auto rental office. I had made arrangement from Oklahoma prior to our trip to pick up a car in England. The clerk asked for my ID and upon seeing my birth date apologized for a slip up on their part because England had passed a law two years earlier preventing them from renting a car to anyone over 70 years of age. Wham!!!! What were we going to do if we didn't have wheels. Our cabbie said, "Mate, I know where you can get a car." He drove us to a used car dealer who said he had a whole lot of used cars and didn't care if they went on the ferry or through the tunnel under the English Channel to France. All he needed was assurance that we had liability insurance. "Don't worry about any dents, just enjoy yourselves." I phoned our insurance company in San Antonio and was assured that we had $50,000 of liability coverage. Problem was solved and we loaded our small bags and hit the road. Our first stop was at Cambridge, England at a beautiful American Soldiers Cemetery. Over 5000 white crosses covered the entire landscape. I found the name of one of my high school buddies and Billie found two friends of hers that were killed in World War II. We both choked up several times while at that spot. To hear our President (2009/2010) apologize to the world for the actions of the United States is disgraceful. The office, at Cambridge, contained a photograph book of all the Military Cemeteries of Americans killed in World Wars I and II, helping our "Allies" rid themselves of tyranny. General Patton is buried in the Luxembourg Cemetery and we did not know that during our time there. He elected to be buried with his troops. A genuine LEADER, not those of today who throw their troops to the winds for Politically Correctness!!!

Our destination in London was the Victory Hotel which was the center of the United Services Organization of WW II. It is located in the heart of London with some 300 or more rooms for active and retired military personnel. The nightly rate is a tenth of the surrounding hotel rates. We were advised to hire a "Black Taxi" as the best way to see the highlights of London. Buckingham Palace was the first stop, The flag was not flying which meant the Queen was out of the country. The golden gates were closed and the guards were marching back and forth. Trafalgar Square with the huge steel lions molded from the melted down ships guns adorned the area which was also covered with bird droppings and thousands of pigeons flitting around. In the distance Big Ben could be seen. From there Piccadilly Circus and the SOHO area was described as a scene of weekend gatherings. The Admiralty Arches and Number 10 Downing Street was visited followed by Westminster Abby. The guide pointed out that the yellow colored bricks were the original building and were 1100 years old. The White bricks were later additions. The House of Commons and Parliament were shown and it was explained that the Queen visited to open each session and had to obtain permission when she wanted to leave the country. We crossed the Thames and picked up a few souvenirs for the kids on our way to the beginnings of London by the Romans in 53AD at Pudding Lane. A quick trip across the newly built bridge that replaced the one sold brick by brick and shipped to Lake Havasu, followed by a return across the London Tower Bridge, with a stop at London Tower which was built in 1070 AD, was the highlight of the tour. The driver recommended that we return to London tower in the late afternoon to take the tour through the buildings. We finished our Taxi tour with a stop by St. Paul's Cathedral where Princess Di and Charles were wed. After a quick bite we retrieved our car and returned to London Tower. Inside a huge vaulted room on a moving sidewalk along a thick glass case enclosing all the Crown Jewels associated with the Kingdom of England, you could hear gasps of wonder from the visitors. Another large glass case contained a Gold Punch Bowl standing on it's pedestal and measuring about five feet long and three feet wide. Artificial replicas of the jewelry were for sale. We were thoroughly worn out and after a nice supper retired to the room for the next adventure in the morning.

England is like the United States, motels are available for stop over, without expensive hotels at high rates such as we encountered in France. We headed to the northeast through industrial Birmingham with a stop over at Oxford for lunch, past Stratford on the Avon and into Wales. Our destination was Ireland and to get there we had to cross the Irish Sea from a small port named Holyhead. I was expecting a small ferry boat such as is used to cross the Mississippi river. (Memories of our river boat trip) To my surprise the ferry boat was as large as our Navy Escort Carriers. Eleven decks high and about 600 feet long with the four lower decks for semi-trucks and autos. Numerous bars, game room for the kids, dinning rooms, cabins for truck drivers to rest, helicopter deck, duty free shopping center, observation deck, elevators and beautiful stair cases. We churned along at about 20 knots for the 60 mile crossing to Dublin. Billie contacted her nationally known Irish Dance Instructor and we were given directions to a competition being held that weekend at the SPA Hotel in Luken about 40 miles out of Dublin. My video camera was not allowed to film the competition but could be used away from the dance floor. We discovered that all those beautiful long curly locks on the Irish Dancers could be purchased in any color desired. Vendors lined the halls with their wares. This was about the time of the Mad Cow Disease and a special on prime rib steak was being offered to rid their supply of beef. We all had a juicy steak that evening. Following the weekend we drove to the instructors studio in Dublin. She was the person who screened all the dancers for the Feet of Flame dance troupe. We watched her classes for several hours and obtained tapes of her dances. We intended to proceed north into Scotland. However a storm was brewing and there had been several bombings recently in Scotland. From Scotland we had intended to return to Mildenhall and catch a flight into Italy. Billie was not feeling good and we boarded the ferry back to Wales and made our way to the Air Base for a flight back to the states.

Everything at home was intact except for fallen leaves that took a week to rake and bag. That fall I bagged 130 39 gallon trash bags of leaves from our property. In November, of that same year 2000, a reunion of all Naval Aviators from the classes of 1950 was held on board Naval Air Station, Pensacola. Class 5-50 had consisted of two battalions of 30 each for a total of 60 cadets. Only six of us attended the reunion. Billie was not feeling well enough to attend the dinner of prime rib that we had ordered. She elected to stay in the hotel room and rest and encouraged me to attend the gathering since it was my reunion. We headed for home after the reunion and for the next two years stayed close to home and stopped further dance classes. The Sooner Clogging Company was turned over to one of the adults and is still active in the year 2010. Billie was under constant medical attention but was gradually getting weaker. At Christmas of 2002 we made our last visit to San Diego to deliver gifts to Mell's family. She felt so bad that had we not sent all those packages to the kids she was ready to turn around and go home. We cut our visit short and returned to Norman. Despite all attempts to cure, she finally developed Leukemia complicated with pneumonia. She slept peacefully away on 20 December 2003. Two days prior to our 52nd anniversary.

Billie was the ultimate in motherhood. She raised her four sons without my every day help and aid during twenty five years of off again/on again home coming and departures during my extensive sea duty as a Naval Aviator. Never complaining and always joyful and inventive of ways to keep her children at the ready for deportment, manners and dress. **SHE DID IT ALL!! SHE WAS A GIVER!!**

DECLINING YEARS

After fifty two years of raising children, constant companionship, clog dancing, shoveling manure and hollering WHOA!!, it gets pretty lonesome around an empty house. I kept busy for two years clearing out every thing I would no longer need. I had invited all the kids in to take what they wanted and started selling off items on Ebay. This kept me occupied on the inside and the yard and pool required my constant attention raking leaves, mowing, and keeping crystal clear swimming water for the grand kids. I again had over 130 bags of leaves after the autumn drop. I had fully expected to precede Billie in death and was surprised that my health and stamina indicated several more years of life. After the second fall leaf raking I decided that I no longer needed to keep that house and large yard. It was getting to be just too much work!! I was growing tired of roaming around the town by myself. As my old friend Junior would say, "I was plum eat up with lonesome!!" I married Billie's second cousin, Rajean. We are happily married in the warm climes of Corpus Christi, TX. No snow to shovel in the winter and no leaves to rake in the fall, four golf courses to keep me busy along with Senior Bowling, constant concerts in town with visiting celebrities, boat shows, and all other forms of entertainment. Billie loved her cousin and I am certain she would be pleased knowing we are keeping each other company.

I have lived through all the Presidents starting with FDR, from the horse and buggy to the Space Station orbiting our planet. From out of doors play after school, until homework, and in the summer til the street lights came on we were running and chasing each other with games to play. Now a large percentage of children sit by the computer playing with their fingers and growing obese to the point that one out of four could no longer pass the physical to serve in the military if needed. Parents are afraid to let their children walk to and from school, to play outside of their own back yard for fear they may be grabbed by some crazed sex maniac roaming the streets that a lawyer and judge has allowed to skirt the law and run free. I drove a school bus for three years prior to Billie's passing because a little six year old had been molested while walking across a field from the bus to his house. I was told not to lay one finger on any student, even to separate a fight, because I could be sued, the bus Manager would be sued, the Principal would be sued, The Superintendent would be sued, for breaking the child's clavicle. Utter nonsense but a fact!!!! The teachers have no authority for fear of a law suit. As a child, if two boys got into a fight and one would kick or hit with a stick or stone or object, he was then shunned by others as a no good dirty fighter. Now the violence on television teaches children to fight dirty, knock them down and then proceed to kick them in the face and head as hard as you can. Violence on TV had destroyed our youth and teaches our citizens how to break the law.

Over these years there has been a gradual and persistent degradation of the freedoms that we used to enjoy. First it was the fourth of July fire cracker elimination because a few idiots failed to observe common sense rules. Punish all because a few are causing a problem. The Lead soldiers and Lead in paint because mothers allowed their children to chew on the window sills and swallow the paint and to put the lead soldiers into their mouths. Parental neglect!! Then the big asbestos scare, then mercury poisoning, then the nut who placed a hot cup of coffee between her legs while driving and suffered second degree buns on you know where. Then along comes the EPA with the intent to clean the rivers and streams and has now burgeoned their noses into every little thing to keep their jobs. Their budget has sky rocketed and every thing is bad for the environment !!!! Next comes OSHA and their little dirt catching fences that within a week have fallen down or been run over, but have caused the builder extra money to erect and added to the cost of homes and buildings. We used to build New York City sky scrapers with no safety nets or harnesses and now can not climb up a ladder without a net to fall into. Unions started out with good intentions and now have increased the price of every manufactured object with all their money grabbing rules and regulations so that our manufacturers have moved out of the country with the resultant loss of jobs for Americans. EPA and OSHA have destroyed our industries with their increased cost regulations and restrictions. Both are out of control. Along comes LBJ and his Executive Order eliminating the immigration quota system. The flood gates are open and our citizens are unemployed because the illegals and multitudes of third world country people will work for less wages. Our Supreme Court ruled that medical aid must be given to any person in stress whether or not they have insurance or are a citizen. Then comes welfare for the lazy and neer-do-wells that breed one illegitimate child after the other and collect food stamps and child support that exceeds the earnings of hard working citizens. My mother was telling her next door neer-do-well that she was sorry to hear of her husbands death. The reply was, "Oh he wont my hubban ah gets da welfare and has plenny munny.!!" Illegal Mexicans cross the border into National City, CA hospital for delivery of their babies for free, and citizenship for the child. Wonderful, the hospital is broke !!!! Smoking freedom is completely out of control, cigarets were two packs for twenty five cents when I was a child and are now up to sixty dollars for a carton of Camels. (Fifty of those dollars are taxes) Now the anti-smokers are trying to prevent a smoker from lighting up outside in a public park. My sister and I used to come down stairs in the morning and the dining room had a nice layer of blue smoke floating across the room from Dad's pipe. Our comment, "Gee that smells good Daddy!!" Mother lived to 87 and I am over 84. Every one smoked, none of my friends have died of lung cancer. Smoking and cancer is like Global Warming and the worst winter season in many years(2010).

All the above subtractions to our freedom are now being compounded by rules and regulations and taxes that put totally unnecessary expenses onto our entrepreneurs. They have been driven overseas to escape the red tape the liberals, lawyers and judges have laid upon them. Now the present (2009/2012) administration is giving free medical care to all the non producers and illegals that have found a way to suck money out of the hard working tax payers, is pushing a Cap and Trade Bill that will increase electrical and fuel costs, wants to grant amnesty to all the millions of illegals already inside our borders, and is encouraging the Muslims to infiltrate our cities and towns with the eventual aim to take over the country. Mosques have grown from 1200 several years ago to well over 2000 to date. A steady infiltration throughout the country. The FBI has recently reported that some IMAMS leading these Mosques are teaching hatred of America and recruiting suicide bombers for attacks within this country.

Through all these losses to our American Way of Life one only has to look at the influence of Lawyers and Judges that are destroying our freedoms. Soon we will be left with no jobs other than services. I am fearful that these incursions into our freedoms have progressed too far to turn the tide back to common sense and logical thought.

Political Correctness has infiltrated every aspect of our lives. It will not be long before we will be unable to enlist young people into the military forces. We have asked our fit youngsters to voluntarily enlist in the military service, have sent them into the cess pools of Iraq and Afghanistan and now are allowing our Military Lawyers to prosecute and imprison them for touching or teasing or killing those that we sent to kill in first place. What mother or father would encourage their children to join the service under these conditions that the Commanders-in-Chief and the Admiral and Generals are allowing to happen. The words of President Bush, "you're either with the terrorists or with us," are being ignored by the liberal right. If the so called "Good Muslims" will not condemn the "Bad Muslims" then they are just as bad and we have no right to send our troops to prison while they hang our people by their heel from a bridge and burn them with gasoline or cut off their heads. Our "Rules of Engagement" are tying the hands of our troops. The Muslim can kill one of our troops, throw his gun down and stand erect, and if one of our men shoot him the JAG Prosecutors will then accuse him of killing and unarmed man and try to send him to prison. Political Correct Bull Crap!!!

Do we think that a huge money crop of opium is going to be replaced with potatoes or corn or lettuce. Now the news reports that we are going to pay the Afghanistan farmers the same amount of money they would have gotten from their opium crop for their tomato crop. How many years into the future would the American tax payer keep up these payments. The first missed payment and back to the Opium crop!! Not a good Idea!!! We are Leaderless!!!! General Pershing ended the uprising in the Philippines by burying the Muslims with pigs. They wanted no part of that and quit the fight. We should have a pig between each prisoner in Guantanamo and when the word got out it would end the fight. Our Leaderless Leaders are allowing the Gitmo terrorists to have a Muslim only room for their Qur'an that the guards are not supposed to enter, signs pointing to Mecca for their prayers, allowed to spit at or on our guards or to throw feces at them with impunity just to satisfy international observers that should not be allowed there in the first place. We are not fighting a war between uniformed military personnel, this is a continuation of the crusades with the intent to drive their foolish religion into all places around the world. The Geneva Convention applies to armed conflict between countries and uniformed armies. It does, in no way, apply to this insurgent type unlawful killing of infidels. The fallacy of becoming a Martyr with 70+ voluptuous virgins in the after life is just plain hog wash. There is no wall of Honor for these idiots that have blown themselves to pieces. The are just **DEAD!!**

As one grows into an octogenarian you realize that when you retire for the night you just might never awaken again. I am into that stage and do not have the stamina to start a campaign preaching against these destructive forces threatening our Great Nation. The voices of the Tea Bagging Express are increasing in strength and I hope the Republican Party and the Tea Baggers join forces so as not to split the ticket in the forthcoming elections. Two publications dissecting the Muslim idiocy are a worthwhile read for Americans:

1. The Politically Incorrect Guide to ISLAM (And the Crusades) by Robert Spencer and

2. The Truth About Muhammad by Robert Spencer

What the press and public officials are afraid to say is put forward in those two books. I understand the author has had to go into seclusion for threats against his life for expounding on the ideology of the Muslim religion.

The Web Site "Overseas Military Cemeteries" provides information on the TWENTY FOUR AMERICAN CEMETERIES in which our troops have been interred in Belgium, France, Italy, Luxembourg, Netherlands, Great Britain, Philippines and Tunisia, Not counting burials at sea. These war deaths were not the result of our aggressive actions but were to defend and assist our allies against outside tyranny by others. This GREAT NATION is always the FIRST to act to assist other nations during earthquake, hurricane, tsunami or other catastrophes. We need not **BOW** or **APOLOGIZE** to any other national leader or nations for our actions PAST or PRESENT.

AMERICANS PLEASE AWAKEN TO THE ATTACK ON YOUR FREEDOMS. WE HAVE A REPRESENTATIVE GOVERNMENT WHERE THE MAJORITY RULES. NOT WHERE A MINORITY SETS THE STANDARDS. WAKE UP! TAKE PART

IN YOUR GOVERNMENT. THE UNITED STATES
IS A CHRISTIAN NATION AND HAS BEEN SINCE
1776. IF A PERSON DOES NOT LIKE OUR WAY OF
LIFE THAT PERSON IS FREE TO **EMIGRATE.**

A rare flight deck accident attributed to Landing Signal Officer's error and Supervisory Error. The LSO said, "My mind said CUT and my hands WAVED OFF. It was my fault." As shown the tail hook had grabbed the cable and the left wing tip and propeller are about to hit the deck. The CUT and WAVE OFF are mandatory. Just "DO IT."

77,000th LANDING ON DECK OF USS VALLEY FORGE

FOUR CANS OF SOUP comprise the larder of the good ship Rollie's Store, bound for New Orleans. Its crew was seeking work in Memphis today. Left to right are Don Strader, Oscar Schaur and Mack Martin.

Chop Cotton To Finance Rowboat Trip

MEMPHIS, TENN., July 5.—Aboard New Orleans Rowboat Expedition—

Only four cans of soup are left.

Three paddling Huckleberry Finn students from the Ohio State University in Columbus, O., are seeking work here to finance the rest of their 2000-mile rowboat trip down the Mississippi to New Orleans.

They're Don Strader, 144 W. Woodruff-av.; Mack Martin, 342 Seymour-av., and Oscar Schafer, 1464 Bryden-rd.

The youths, who left Columbus Monday, June 16, are negotiating the muddy Mississippi with the aid of good oars. They ...

Columbus, Ohio Dispatch newspaper clipping following the adventures of the three Navy veterans rowboat trip from Columbus to New Orleans in summer of 1947.

Billie's group photo of her clogging students during their performance in Norma, OK at a Moose Club gathering.

Hunter/Killer Team of the AF2W (No. 11) and AF2S (No.6) Single Piloted Aircraft with two Air Crewman on a search mission hunting submarines off the coast of the United States during the early 1950's.

VS 24 Duty Cat Patch is awarded to those pilots both day and night carrier qualified in the AF Anti-Submarine Warfare aircraft. The bolt of lightning symbolized a night catapult shot into the inky blackness. The AF aircraft was the largest single engine stick aircraft operating off the smallest carriers during the early to late 1950's.

Photo of the AF2S taken at the Pensacola Aviation Museum showing the relative size of the aircraft in which the pilot sits 13 feet above the flight deck.

Commander Cruiser/Destroyer Flotilla THREE awarding CDR Schaer the Bronze Star for his services with the SEVENTH FLEET during the Vietnam Conflict 1968.

CDR Schaer being initiated into the realm of King Neptune during the Equator Crossing in 1968. From a "Pollywog" to a "Shell Back" and old naval tradition.